PRAISE FOR *HEAVEN IS FOR REAL*

"You will be moved by the honest, simple, childlike accounts of a little boy who has been to heaven. It's compelling and convincing. It's a book you should read. If you're ready to go to heaven, this book will inspire you. If you're not ready for heaven, allow a little child to lead you. Like Colton says, *Heaven Is for Real.*"

— Don Piper
Speaker and Author, *90 Minutes in Heaven*

"Every now and again a manuscript comes across my desk where the title intrigues me. That's what happened with this particular book called *Heaven Is for Real*. I thought I'd just skim through it, but I couldn't put it down. I read it from cover to cover. I was so impacted by the story. It's a book that will not only make you love God more and fear death less, but it will help you understand that heaven is not a place where we just sit around for a thousand years singing Kumbaya; it's a place where we begin to live as we were always meant to live, before the fall. If heaven is something that intrigues you, or troubles you, if you wonder what our lives will be like, then I highly recommend this book."

— Sheila Walsh
WOF Speaker and Author,
Beautiful Things Happen When a Woman Trusts God

"Heaven is not a consolation prize. It is a real place that will be the eternal home for all who believe. Take a journey with Colton and Todd as they describe firsthand the wonders, mysteries, and majesty of heaven. It will make earth more meaningful and the future more hopeful."

— Brady Boyd
Senior Pastor, New Life Church,
Colorado Springs

"There have been many stories of 'near-death' experiences that I simply have not read because I frankly didn't know if I could trust the author. Well, I have read this book cover to cover and, moreover, I could hardly put it down! Why? Because I know the author and I believe him. Todd Burpo gives us a wonderful gift as he and his son lift the veil on eternity, allowing us a quick glimpse of what lies on the other side."

— Dr. Everett Piper
President, Oklahoma Wesleyan
University
Author, *Why I'm a Liberal and Other Conservative Ideas*

"In this beautiful and well-written book, Colton, age four, has an experience consistent with a near-death experience (NDE) while under anesthesia. I have scientifically studied over 1,600 NDEs, and found that typical NDEs may occur in very young children and while under anesthesia. Even after studying so many NDEs, I found Colton's experience to be dramatic, exceptional, and an inspiration to Christians everywhere."

— Jeffrey Long, MD
Founder, Near Death Experience
Research Foundation
Author, *Evidence of the Afterlife: The Science of Near-Death Experiences*

"A beautifully written glimpse into heaven that will encourage those who doubt and thrill those who believe."

— Ron Hall
Coauthor, *Same Kind of Different as Me*

"Some stories want to be told. They simply have a life of their own. The book you hold in your hand is just such a story. But it won't stay long with you; it will bubble over into your conversations in search of someone who has not yet heard. I know it will happen to you because that is what happened to me."

— Phil McCallum
Senior Pastor, Evergreen
Community Church
Bothell, Washington

"The Bible describes heaven as the dwelling place of God. It is a real place that all those who submit their lives to God will have as an eternal dwelling. In this book Todd Burpo relays the account of his son's experience when he was in surgery for a burst appendix. It is honest and touching and encouraging to all of us who have an eternal hope."

— Robert Morris
Pastor, Gateway Church,
Southlake, Texas

"*Heaven Is for Real* is a wonderful book. It reaffirms how important faith is in our lives—for children as well as adults."

— Timothy P. O'Holleran, MD

"Colton's story could have been in the New Testament—but God has chosen to speak to us in this twenty-first century through the unblemished eyes of a child, revealing some of the mysteries of heaven. The writing is compelling and the truth astonishing, creating a hunger for more."

— Jo Anne Lyon
General Superintendent,
The Wesleyan Church

"God is so creative and credible! The discoveries of this book will amplify that in new ways. I've known Colton since birth. As a toddler, he already had a keen spiritual interest and intensity. At about age 3, he sat on my knee, looked me in the eyes and asked if I wanted to go to heaven when I died. Then told me "You need to have Jesus in your heart." I commend this book as a fresh perspective on the reality of God, who often seems hidden yet interrupts on His schedule."

— Phil Harris
District Superintendent,
Colorado-Nebraska District of
the Wesleyan Church

"It is always a blessing to hear that Akiane's paintings have touched another person's life. Her *Prince of Peace* depiction of Christ remains one of her most beloved works. And as parents of a child that has experienced something extraordinary and unexplained by earthly measures, I celebrate with this family in their joy and in the telling of their special story."

— Forelli Kramarik
Coauthor, *Akiane: Her Life,*
Her Heart, Her Poetry

Heaven Is for Real

Heaven Is for Real

A Little Boy's Astounding Story of His Trip to Heaven and Back

---

INCLUDING CONVERSATION GUIDE

Todd Burpo

with Lynn Vincent

THOMAS NELSON

Since 1798

NASHVILLE   DALLAS   MEXICO CITY   RIO DE JANEIRO

Published in Nashville, Tennessee, by Thomas Nelson. Thomas Nelson is a registered trademark of Thomas Nelson, Inc.

Author is represented by the literary agency of Alive Communications, Inc., 7680 Goddard Street, Suite 200, Colorado Springs, CO 80920.

Thomas Nelson, Inc., titles may be purchased in bulk for educational, business, fund-raising, or sales promotional use. For information, please e-mail SpecialMarkets@ThomasNelson.com.

Unless otherwise noted, Scripture quotations are taken from the HOLY BIBLE: NEW INTERNATIONAL VERSION®. © 1973, 1978, 1984 by International Bible Society. Used by permission of Zondervan Publishing House. All rights reserved.

Scripture quotations marked NLT are taken from *Holy Bible*, New Living Translation. © 1996, 2004. Used by permission of Tyndale House Publishers, Inc., Wheaton, Illinois 60189. All rights reserved.

Scripture quotations marked ESV are taken from THE ENGLISH STANDARD VERSION. © 2001 by Crossway Bibles, a division of Good News Publishers.

Scripture quotations marked NKJV are taken from THE NEW KING JAMES VERSION. © 1982 by Thomas Nelson, Inc. Used by permission. All rights reserved.

Scripture quotations marked KJV are taken from the King James Version of the Bible. Public domain.

ISBN 978-0-7852-3826-3 (with Conversation Guide)
ISBN 978-1-4041-7542-6 (TBN)

Library of Congress Cataloging-in-Publication Data

Burpo, Todd.
    Heaven is for real : a little boy's astounding story of his trip to heaven and back / Todd Burpo with Lynn Vincent.
        p. cm.
    Includes bibliographical references (p. 159).
    ISBN 978-0-8499-4615-8 (pbk.)
    1. Heaven—Christianity. 2. Burpo, Colton, 1999– 3. Near-death experiences—Religious aspects—Christianity. I. Vincent, Lynn. II. Title.
BT846.3.B87 2010
133.901'3092—dc22   2010023391

Printed in the United States of America

12 13 14 15 16   QG   5 4 3 2 1

"I tell you the truth, unless you change and become like little children, you will never enter the kingdom of heaven."

—JESUS OF NAZARETH

CONTENTS

ACKNOWLEDGMENTS

In telling Colton's story, we have been afforded the chance to not just work with dedicated professionals but with real and caring people. Sure, we have been impressed with their expertise, but Sonja and I have been more delighted by their character and their hearts.

Phil McCallum, Joel Kneedler, Lynn Vincent, and Debbie Wickwire have not just invested their own lives into the making of this book; they have also enriched our family. Without their enormous efforts and sensitive spirits, *Heaven Is For Real* would have never developed so wonderfully.

We thank God daily for assembling these gifted and talented people to help us tell Colton's story. Each one has been a blessing to us.

Sonja and I count it a wonderful privilege to call them our friends.

PROLOGUE

Angels at Arby's

The Fourth of July holiday calls up memories of patriotic parades, the savory scents of smoky barbecue, sweet corn, and night skies bursting with showers of light. But for my family, the July Fourth weekend of 2003 was a big deal for other reasons.

My wife, Sonja, and I had planned to take the kids to visit Sonja's brother, Steve, and his family in Sioux Falls, South Dakota. It would be our first chance to meet our nephew, Bennett, born two months earlier. Plus, our kids, Cassie and Colton, had never been to the falls before. (Yes, there really is a Sioux Falls in Sioux Falls.) But the biggest deal of all was this: this trip would be the first time we'd left our hometown of Imperial, Nebraska, since a family trip to Greeley, Colorado, in March had turned into the worst nightmare of our lives.

To put it bluntly, the last time we had taken a family trip, one of our children almost died. Call us crazy, but we were a little apprehensive this time, almost to the point of not wanting to go. Now, as a pastor, I'm not a believer in superstition. Still, some weird, unsettled part of me felt that if we just hunkered down close to home, we'd be safe. Finally, though, reason—and the lure of meeting little Bennett, whom Steve had told us was the world's cutest baby—won out. So we packed up a weekend's worth of paraphernalia in our blue Ford Expedition and got our family ready to head north.

Sonja and I decided the best plan would be to get most of the driving done at night. That way, even though Colton would be strapped into his car seat against his four-year-old, I'm-a-big-kid will, at least he'd sleep for most of the trip. So it was a little after 8 p.m. when I backed the Expedition out of our driveway, steered past Crossroads Wesleyan Church, my pastorate, and hit Highway 61.

The night spread clear and bright across the plains, a half moon white against a velvet sky. Imperial is a small farming town tucked just inside the western border of Nebraska. With only two thousand souls and zero traffic lights, it's the kind of town with more churches than banks, where farmers stream straight off the fields into the family-owned café at lunchtime, wearing Wolverine work boots, John Deere ball caps, and a pair of pliers for fence-mending hanging off their hips. So Cassie, age six, and Colton were excited to be on the road to the "big city" of Sioux Falls to meet their newborn cousin.

The kids chattered for ninety miles to the city of North Platte, with Colton fighting action-figure superhero battles and saving the world several times on the way. It wasn't quite 10 p.m. when we pulled into the town of about twenty-four thousand, whose greatest claim to fame is that it was the hometown of the famous Wild West showman, Buffalo Bill Cody. North Platte would be about the last civilized stop—or at least the last *open* stop—we'd pass that night as we headed northeast across vast stretches of cornfields empty of everything but deer, pheasant, and an occasional farmhouse. We had planned in advance to stop there to top off both the gas tank and our bellies.

After a fill-up at a Sinclair gas station, we pulled out onto Jeffers Street, and I noticed we were passing through the traffic light where, if we turned left, we'd wind up at the Great Plains Regional Medical Center. That was where we'd spent fifteen nightmarish days in March, much of it on our knees, praying for God to spare Colton's life. God did, but Sonja and I joke that the experience shaved years off our own lives.

Sometimes laughter is the only way to process tough times, so as we passed the turnoff, I decided to rib Colton a little.

"Hey, Colton, if we turn here, we can go back to the hospital," I said. "Do you wanna go back to the hospital?"

Our preschooler giggled in the dark. "No, Daddy, don't send me! Send Cassie . . . Cassie can go to the hospital!"

Sitting next to him, his sister laughed. "Nuh-*uh*! I don't wanna go either!"

In the passenger seat, Sonja turned so that she could see our son, whose car seat was parked behind mine. I pictured his blond crew cut and his sky-blue eyes shining in the dark. "Do you remember the hospital, Colton?" Sonja said.

"Yes, Mommy, I remember," he said. "That's where the angels sang to me."

Inside the Expedition, time froze. Sonja and I looked at each other, passing a silent message: *Did he just say what I think he said?*

Sonja leaned over and whispered, "Has he talked to you about angels before?"

I shook my head. "You?"

She shook her head.

I spotted an Arby's, pulled into the parking lot, and switched off the engine. White light from a street lamp filtered into the Expedition. Twisting in my seat, I peered back at Colton. In that moment, I was struck by his smallness, his little boyness. He was really just a little guy who still spoke with an endearing (and sometimes embarrassing) call-it-like-you-see-it innocence. If you're a parent, you know what I mean: the age where a kid might point to a pregnant woman and ask (very loudly), "Daddy, why is that lady so fat?" Colton was in that narrow window of life where he hadn't yet learned either tact or guile.

All these thoughts flashed through my mind as I tried to figure how to respond to my four-year-old's simple proclamation that *angels* had sung to him. Finally, I plunged in: "Colton, you said that angels sang to you while you were at the hospital?"

He nodded his head vigorously.

"What did they sing to you?"

Colton turned his eyes up and to the right, the attitude of remembering. "Well, they sang 'Jesus Loves Me' and 'Joshua Fought the Battle of Jericho,'" he said earnestly. "I asked them to sing 'We Will, We Will Rock You,' but they wouldn't sing that."

As Cassie giggled softly, I noticed that Colton's answer had been quick and matter-of-fact, without a hint of hesitation.

Sonja and I exchanged glances again. *What's going on? Did he have a dream in the hospital?*

And one more unspoken question: *What do we say now?*

A natural question popped into my head: "Colton, what did the angels look like?"

He chuckled at what seemed to be a memory. "Well, one of them looked like Grandpa Dennis, but it wasn't him, 'cause Grandpa Dennis has glasses."

Then he grew serious. "Dad, Jesus had the angels sing to me because I was so scared. They made me feel better."

Jesus?

I glanced at Sonja again and saw that her mouth had dropped open. I turned back to Colton. "You mean Jesus was there?"

My little boy nodded as though reporting nothing more remarkable than seeing a ladybug in the front yard. "Yeah, Jesus was there."

"Well, where was Jesus?"

Colton looked me right in the eye. "I was sitting in Jesus' lap."

If there are Stop buttons on conversations, that was one of them right there. Astonished into speechlessness, Sonja and I looked at each other and passed another silent telegram: *Okay, we really need to talk about this.*

We all piled out of the Expedition and trooped into Arby's, emerging a few minutes later with a bag of grub. In between, Sonja and I exchanged whispers.

"Do you think he really saw angels?"

"And *Jesus*?!"

"I don't know."

"Was it a dream?"

"I don't know—he seems so sure."

Back in the SUV, Sonja passed out roast beef sandwiches and potato cakes, and I ventured another question.

"Colton, where were you when you saw Jesus?"

He looked at me as if to say, *Didn't we just talk about this?*

"At the hospital. You know, when Dr. O'Holleran was working on me."

"Well, Dr. O'Holleran worked on you a couple of times, remember?" I said. Colton had both an emergency appendectomy and then an abdominal clean-out in the hospital, and later we had taken Colton to have some keloid scarring removed, but that was at Dr. O'Holleran's office. "Are you sure it was at the hospital?"

Colton nodded. "Yeah, at the hospital. When I was with Jesus, you were praying, and Mommy was talking on the phone."

What?

That definitely meant he was talking about the hospital. But how in the world did he know where we had been?

"But you were in the operating room, Colton," I said. "How could you know what we were doing?"

"'Cause I could see you," Colton said matter-of-factly. "I went up out of my body and I was looking down and I could see the doctor working on my body. And I saw you and Mommy. You were in a little room by yourself, praying; and

Mommy was in a different room, and she was praying and talking on the phone."

Colton's words rocked me to my core. Sonja's eyes were wider than ever, but she said nothing, just stared at me and absently bit into her sandwich.

That was all the information I could handle at that point. I started the engine, steered the Expedition back onto the street, and pointed us toward South Dakota. As I hit I-80, pasturelands unrolled on either side, dotted here and there with duck ponds that glinted in the moonlight. By then, it was very late, and soon everyone else was snoozing as planned.

As the road hummed underneath me, I marveled at the things I had just heard. Our little boy had said some pretty incredible stuff—and he had backed it up with credible information, things there was no way he could have known. We had not told him what we were doing while he was in surgery, under anesthesia, apparently unconscious.

Over and over, I kept asking myself, *How could he have known?* But by the time we rolled across the South Dakota state line, I had another question: *Could this be real?*

ONE

THE CRAWL—A—SEE—UM

The family trip when our nightmare began was supposed to be a celebration. In early March 2003, I was scheduled to travel to Greeley, Colorado, for a district board meeting of the Wesleyan church. Beginning the August before, our family had traveled a rocky road: seven months of back-to-back injury and illness that included a shattered leg, two surgeries, and a cancer scare, all of which combined to drain our bank account to the point where I could almost hear sucking sounds when the statements came in the mail. My small pastor's salary hadn't been affected, but our financial mainstay was the overhead garage door business we owned. Our medical trials had taken a heavy toll.

By February, though, we seemed to be on the other side of all that. Since I had to travel anyway, we decided to turn the board-meeting trip into a kind of marker in our family life—a time to have a little fun, revive our minds and spirits, and start moving forward again with fresh hope.

Sonja had heard of a neat place for kids to visit just outside

Denver called the Butterfly Pavilion. Billed as an "invertebrate zoo," the Butterfly Pavilion opened in 1995 as an educational project that would teach people about the wonders of insects as well as marine critters, the kinds that live in tide pools. These days, kids are greeted outside the zoo by a towering and colorful metal sculpture of a praying mantis. But back in 2003, the giant insect hadn't taken up his post yet, so the low brick building about fifteen minutes from downtown Denver didn't shout "Kid appeal!" on the outside. But inside, a world of wonders waited, especially for kids Colton's and Cassie's ages.

The first place we stopped was the "Crawl-A-See-Um," a room filled with terrariums housing creepy-crawly critters from beetles to roaches to spiders. One exhibit, the Tarantula Tower, drew Cassie and Colton like a magnet. This stack of terrariums was, exactly as advertised, a tower of glassed-in habitats containing the kind of furry, thick-legged spiders that either fascinate you or give you the willies.

Cassie and Colton took turns climbing a three-step folding stool in order to get a look at the residents of the Tarantula Tower's upper stories. In one terrarium, a Mexican blonde tarantula squatted in a corner, its exoskeleton covered with what the exhibit placard described as hair in a "lovely" pale color. Another habitat contained a red-and-black tarantula native to India. One of the scarier-looking residents was a "skeleton tarantula," so named because its black legs were segmented with white bands so that the spider looked a little like an Xray in reverse. We later heard that this particular skeleton tarantula was a bit of a rebel: once, she had somehow engineered a jailbreak, invaded the habitat next door, and eaten her neighbor for lunch.

As Colton hopped up on the footstool to see what the rogue tarantula looked like, he glanced back at me with a grin that warmed me. I could feel my neck muscles begin to unknot, and somewhere inside me a pressure valve released, the emotional equivalent of a long sigh. For the first time in months, I felt I could simply enjoy my family.

"Wow, look at that one!" Cassie said, pointing into one of the terrariums. A slightly gangly six-year-old, my daughter was as smart as a whip, a trait she got from her mom. Cassie was pointing to the exhibit sign, which read: "Goliath Birdeater . . . females can be over eleven inches long."

The one in this tank was only about six inches long, but its body was as thick as Colton's wrist. He stared through the glass wide-eyed. I looked over and saw Sonja wrinkle her nose.

I guess one of the volunteer zookeepers saw her expression, too, because he quickly came to the birdeater's defense. "The Goliath is from South America," he said in a friendly, educational tone that said, *They're not as yucky as you think.* "Tarantulas from North and South America are very docile. You can even hold one right over there." He pointed to where another zookeeper was holding a smaller tarantula in his palm so that a group of kids could take a closer look.

Cassie darted across the room to see what all the fuss was about, with Sonja, Colton, and me bringing up the rear. In a corner of the room decorated to look like a bamboo hut, the keeper was displaying the undisputed star of the

Crawl-A-See-Um, Rosie the Spider. A rose-haired tarantula from South America, Rosie was a furry arachnid with a plum-size body and legs six inches long, thick as pencils. But the best thing about Rosie from a kid's point of view was that if you were brave enough to hold her, even for a moment, the zookeeper would award you with a sticker.

Now, if you have little kids, you already know that there are times they'd rather have a good sticker than a handful of cash. And this sticker was special: white with a picture of a tarantula stamped in yellow, it read, "I held Rosie!"

This wasn't just any old sticker; this was a badge of courage!

Cassie bent low over the keeper's hand. Colton looked up at me, blue eyes wide. "Can I have a sticker, Daddy?"

"You have to hold Rosie to get a sticker, buddy."

At that age, Colton had this precious way of talking, part-serious, part-breathless, golly-gee wonder. He was a smart, funny little guy with a black-and-white way of looking at life. Something was either fun (LEGOs) or it wasn't (Barbies). He either liked food (steak) or hated it (green beans). There were good guys and bad guys, and his favorite toys were good-guy action figures. Superheroes were a big deal to Colton. He took his Spider-Man, Batman, and Buzz Lightyear action figures with him everywhere he went. That way, whether he was stuck in the backseat of the SUV, in a waiting room, or on the floor at the church, he could still create scenes in which the good guys saved the world. This usually involved swords, Colton's favorite weapon for banishing evil. At home, he could *be* the superhero. I'd often walk into the house and find Colton armed to the teeth, a toy sword tucked through each side of his belt and one in each hand: "I'm playing Zorro, Daddy! Wanna play?"

Now Colton turned his gaze to the spider in the keeper's hand, and it looked to me like he wished he had a sword right then, at least for moral support. I tried to imagine how huge the spider must look to a little guy who wasn't even four feet tall. Our son was all boy—a rough-and-tumble kid who had gotten up close and personal with plenty of ants and beetles and other crawling creatures. But none of those creepy-crawlies had been as big as his face and with hair nearly as long as his own.

Cassie straightened and smiled at Sonja. "I'll hold her, Mommy. Can I hold Rosie?"

"Okay, but you'll have to wait your turn," Sonja said.

Cassie got in line behind a couple of other kids. Colton's eyes never left Rosie as first a boy then a girl held the enormous spider and the zookeeper awarded the coveted stickers. In no time at all, Cassie's moment of truth arrived. Colton braced himself against my legs, close enough to see his sister, but trying to bolt at the same time, pushing back against my knees. Cassie held out her palm and we all watched as Rosie, an old hand with small, curious humans, lifted one furry leg at a time and scurried across the bridge from the keeper's hand into Cassie's, then back into the keeper's.

"You did it!" the keeper said as Sonja and I clapped and cheered. "Good job!" Then the zookeeper stood, peeled a white-and-yellow sticker off a big roll, and gave it to Cassie.

This, of course, made it even worse for Colton, who had

not only been upstaged by his sister but was now also the only stickerless Burpo kid. He gazed longingly at Cassie's prize, then back at Rosie, and I could see him trying to wrestle down his fear. Finally, he pursed his lips, dragged his gaze away from Rosie, and looked back up at me. "I don't want to hold her."

"Okay," I said.

"But can I have a sticker?"

"Nope, the only way to get one is to hold her. Cassie did it. You can do it if you want to. Do you want to try? Just for a second?"

Colton looked back at the spider, then at his sister, and I could see wheels turning behind his eyes: *Cassie did it. She didn't get bit.*

Then he shook his head firmly: No. "But I *still* want a *sticker!*" he insisted. At the time, Colton was two months shy of four years old—and he was very good at standing his ground.

"The only way you can get a sticker is if you hold Rosie," Sonja said. "Are you sure you don't want to hold her?"

Colton answered by grabbing Sonja's hand and trying to tug her away from the keeper. "No. I wanna to go see the starfish."

"Are you sure?" Sonja said.

With a vigorous nod, Colton marched toward the Crawl-A-See-Um door.

TWO

PASTOR JOB

In the next room, we found rows of aquariums and indoor "tide pools." We wandered around the exhibits, taking in starfish and mollusks and sea anemones that looked like underwater blossoms. Cassie and Colton oohed and aahed as they dipped their hands in man-made tide pools and touched creatures that they had never seen.

Next, we stepped into a massive atrium, bursting with jungle leaves, vines tumbling down, branches climbing toward the sky. I took in the palm trees and exotic flowers that looked as if they'd come from one of Colton's storybooks. And all around us, clouds of butterflies flitted and swirled.

As the kids explored, I let my mind drift back to the summer before, when Sonja and I played in a coed softball league, like we do every year. We usually finished in the top five, even though we played on the "old folks" team—translation: people in their thirties—battling teams made up of college kids. Now it struck me as ironic that our family's seven-month trial began with an injury that occurred in the last game of our last tournament of the 2002 season. I played center field, and Sonja played outfield rover. By then, Sonja had earned her master's degree in library science and to me was even more beautiful than when she'd first caught my eye as a freshman strolling across the quad at Bartlesville Wesleyan College.

Summer was winding down, but the dog days of the season were in full force with a penetrating heat, thirsty for rain. We had traveled from Imperial about twenty miles down the road to the village of Wauneta for a double-elimination tournament. At nearly midnight, we were battling our way up through the bracket, playing under the blue-white glow of the field lights.

I don't remember what the score was, but I remember we were at the tail end of the game and the lead was within reach. I had hit a double and was perched on second base. Our next batter came up and knocked a pitch that landed in the center-field grass. I saw my chance. As an outfielder ran to scoop up the ball, I took off for third base.

I sensed the ball winging toward the infield.

Our third-base coach motioned frantically: "Slide! Slide!"

Adrenaline pumping, I dropped to the ground and felt the red dirt swooshing underneath my left hip. The other team's third baseman stretched out his glove hand for the ball and—

Crack!

The sound of my leg breaking was so loud that I imagined the ball had zinged in from the outfield and smacked it. Fire exploded in my shin and ankle. I fell to my back, contracted into a fetal position, and pulled my knee up to my belly. The pain was searing, and I remember the dirt around me transforming into a blur of legs, then concerned faces, as two of our players, both EMTs, ran to my aid.

I dimly remember Sonja rushing over to take a look. I could tell by her expression that my leg was bent in ways that didn't look natural. She stepped back to let our EMT friends get to work. A twenty-mile ride later, hospital Xrays revealed a pair of nasty breaks. The tibia, the larger bone in my lower leg, had sustained what doctors call a "spiral break," meaning that each end of the break looked like the barber-pole pattern on a drill bit. Also, my ankle had snapped completely in half. That was probably the break I had heard. I later learned that the cracking sound was so loud that people sitting in the stands at first base heard it.

That sound replayed in my head as Sonja and I watched Cassie and Colton scamper ahead of us in the Butterfly Pavilion atrium. The kids stopped on a small bridge and peered down into a koi pond, chattering and pointing. Clouds of butterflies floated around us, and I glanced at the brochure I'd bought at the front desk to see if I could tell their names. There were "blue morphos" with wings a deep aquamarine, black-and-white "paper kites" that flew slowly and gently like snippets of newsprint floating down through the air, and the "cloudless sulfur," a tropical butterfly with wings the color of fresh mango.

At this point, I was just happy to finally be able to walk without a limp. Besides the hacksaw pain of the spiral break, the most immediate effect of my accident was financial. It's pretty tough to climb up and down ladders to install garage doors while dragging a ten-pound cast and a knee that won't bend. Our bank balance took a sudden and rapid nosedive.

On a blue-collar pastor's salary, what little reserve we had evaporated within weeks. Meanwhile, the amount we had coming in was chopped in half.

The pain of that went beyond money, though. I served as both a volunteer firefighter and high school wrestling coach, commitments that suffered because of my bum leg. Sundays became a challenge too. I'm one of those pastors who walks back and forth during the sermon. Not a holy-rolling, fire-and-brimstone guy by any stretch, but not a soft-spoken minister in vestments, performing liturgical readings either. I'm a story-teller, and to tell stories I need to move around some. But now I had to preach sitting down with my leg propped in a second chair, sticking out like the jib sail. Asking me to sit down while I delivered the Sunday message was like asking an Italian to talk without using his hands. But as much as I struggled with the inconvenience of my injury, I didn't know then that it would be only the first domino to fall.

One morning that October, right about the time I'd got-ten used to hobbling everywhere on crutches, I awoke to a dull throbbing in my lower back. I knew instantly what the problem was: kidney stones.

The first time I had a kidney stone, it measured six milli-meters and required surgery. This time after a round of tests, doctors thought the stones were small enough to pass. I don't know whether that was a good thing, though: I passed them for three days. I had once slammed my middle finger in a tailgate and cut the tip off. That was like baking cookies com-pared to this. Even breaking my leg into four pieces hadn't hurt as bad.

Still, I survived. By November, I'd been hobbling around on crutches for three months, and I went in for a checkup.

"The leg's healing correctly, but we still need to keep it casted," the orthopedist said. "Anything else bothering you?"

Actually, there was. I felt a little weird bringing it up, but the left side of my chest had developed a knot right beneath the surface of the nipple. I'm right-handed and had been leaning on my left crutch a lot while writing, so I thought maybe the underarm pad on that crutch had rubbed against my chest over a period of weeks, creating some kind of irritation beneath the skin, a callus of some kind.

The doctor immediately ruled that out. "Crutches don't do that," he said. "I need to call a surgeon."

The surgeon, Dr. Timothy O'Holleran, performed a needle biopsy. The results that came back a few days later shocked me: hyperplasia. Translation: the precursor to breast cancer.

Breast cancer! A man with a broken leg, kidney stones, and—come on, really?—*breast cancer?*

Later, when other pastors in my district got wind of it, they started calling me Pastor Job, after the man in the biblical book of the same name who was struck with a series of increasingly bizarre symptoms. For now, though, the surgeon ordered the same thing he would've if a woman's biopsy had come back with the same results: a lumpectomy.

Strong, Midwestern woman that she is, Sonja took a practical approach to the news. If surgery was what the doctor ordered, that's the path we would walk. We'd get through it, as a family.

I felt the same way. But it was also about this time that I

also started feeling sorry for myself. For one thing, I was tired of loping around on crutches. Also, a lumpectomy isn't exactly the manliest surgery in the world. Finally, I'd been asking the church board for a long time to set aside money for me for an assistant. Only after this second round of kidney stones did the board vote to authorize the position.

Instead of feeling grateful as I should have, I indulged myself with resentment: *So I have to be a cripple* and *be on the verge of a cancer diagnosis to get a little help around here?*

My pity party really got rolling one afternoon. I was down on the first floor of the church property, a finished basement, really, where we had a kitchen, a classroom, and a large fellowship area. I had just finished up some paperwork and began working my way upstairs on my crutches. Down at the bottom, on the first step, I started getting mad at God.

"This isn't fair," I grumbled aloud, as I struggled up the stairs, one crutch at a time, one step at a time. "I have to suffer and be in this pathetic state for them to give me the help I've needed all along."

Feeling pretty smug in my martyrdom, I had just reached the top landing when a still, small voice arose in my heart: *And what did my Son do for you?*

Humbled and ashamed of my selfishness, I remembered what Jesus said to the disciples: "A student is not above his teacher, nor a servant above his master."[1] Sure, I'd had a rough few months, but they were nothing compared with what a lot of people in the world were going through, even at that very minute. God had blessed me with a small group of believers whom I was charged to shepherd and serve, and here I was griping at God because those believers weren't serving me.

"Lord, forgive me," I said, and swung forward with renewed strength, as if my crutches were eagles' wings.

The truth was, my church *was* serving me—loving me through a special time of prayer they'd set aside. One morning in the beginning of December, Dr. O'Holleran called me at home with strange news: not only was the tissue benign; it was entirely normal. Normal breast tissue. "I can't explain why," he said. "The biopsy definitely showed hyperplasia, so we would expect to see the same thing in the breast tissue removed during the lumpectomy. But the tissue was completely normal. I don't know what to say. I don't know how that happened."

I knew: God had loved me with a little miracle.

THREE

COLTON TOUGHS IT OUT

That next month, the cast came off. With the cancer scare and kidney stones behind us, I spent a couple of months learning to walk again, first with a walking cast, then with a pretty nasty limp, slowly working my atrophied muscles back to health again. By February, I finally achieved some independence—just in time for a district board meeting of our church denomination in Greeley, Colorado, set for the first week in March.

"You need to get away," Sonja told me a couple of weeks before the board meeting. "Just get away and have a little fun."

Now, here we were at the Butterfly Pavilion. A monarch butterfly fluttered past, its bright orange wings segmented in black like stained glass. I breathed a prayer of thanks that our trip had happened at all.

Two days before, on Thursday, Colton had begun telling Sonja that his stomach hurt. I was already in Greeley, and at the time, Sonja was teaching a Title 1 class at Imperial High School. Not wanting to put the school to the expense of a substitute, she asked our good friend Norma Dannatt if she could watch Colton at her home so that Sonja could go to work. Norma, who was like a favorite aunt to our kids, immediately said yes. But at midday, Sonja's cell phone rang. It was Norma: Colton's condition had taken a nosedive. He had a fever with chills and for most of the morning had lain nearly motionless on Norma's couch, wrapped in a blanket.

"He says he's freezing, but he's sweating like crazy," Norma said, clearly concerned. She said Colton's forehead was covered in beads of sweat as big as teardrops.

Norma's husband, Bryan, had come home, taken one look, and decided Colton was sick enough that he should go to the emergency room. Sonja called me in Greeley with the news, and just like that, I saw our trip to celebrate the end of a string of injury and illness being cancelled by . . . illness.

Sonja checked out of work early, scooped up Colton from Norma's house, and took him to the doctor, who revealed that a stomach flu was working its way around town. Through that night, our trip remained up in the air. Separately, in Greeley and Imperial, Sonja and I prayed that Colton would feel well enough to make the trip and by morning, we got our answer: yes!

During the night, Colton's fever broke and by afternoon on Friday, he was his old self again. Sonja called to tell me: "We're on our way!"

Now, at the Butterfly Pavilion, Sonja checked her watch. We were scheduled to meet Steve Wilson, the pastor of Greeley Wesleyan Church, and his wife, Rebecca, for dinner that evening, and the kids still wanted to get in a swim at the hotel pool. There was *zero* chance of them swimming in Imperial in March, so this was a rare opportunity. "Okay, we should probably head back to the hotel," Sonja said.

I looked at her and then at Colton. "Hey, bud, it's time to go. Are you still sure you don't want to hold Rosie?" I said. "Last chance to get a sticker. What do you think?"

Emotions played over Colton's face like sunshine and clouds in a fast-moving weather front. By now, even his big sister had been ribbing him a little about being afraid. As I watched, Colton narrowed his eyes and set his jaw: he wanted that sticker.

"Okay, I'll hold her," he said. "But just for a little bit."

Before he could change his mind, we all trooped back into the Crawl-A-See-Um, and I corralled the keeper. "This is Colton, and he wants to give it a try," I said.

The keeper smiled and bent down. "Okay, Colton, are you ready?"

Stiff as a board, our son held out his hand, and I bent over and cradled it in my own.

"Now, this is super easy, Colton," the keeper said. "Just hold your hand out flat and still. Rosie is very gentle. She won't hurt you."

The keeper raised his hand, and Rosie sidled over to Colton's hand and back to the keeper's waiting hand on the other side, never even slowing down. We all broke into cheers and clapped for Colton as the keeper handed him his sticker. He had faced his fear! It was a big victory for him. The moment seemed like icing on the cake of a perfect day.

As we left the Butterfly Pavilion, I reflected back over the past several months. It was hard to believe that the broken leg, the kidney stones, the lost work, the financial stress, three surgeries, and the cancer scare had all happened in half a year's time. In that moment, I realized for the first time that I had been feeling like I'd been in a fight. For months, I'd had my guard up, waiting for the next punch life could throw. Now, though, I felt completely relaxed for the first time since the previous summer.

If I'd let my mind roll with that boxing metaphor just a little longer, I might've followed it to its logical conclusion: In a boxing match, the fighters absorb some vicious blows because they're ready for them. And usually, the knockout punch is the one they didn't see coming.

FOUR

SMOKE SIGNALS

Later that evening, with a swim under their belts, Cassie and Colton sat in a big round booth at the Old Chicago Restaurant in Greeley, Colorado, coloring happily while Sonja and I chatted with Pastor Steve Wilson and his wife, Rebecca. We had already chowed down on some terrific Italian food, including the usual kid favorites—pizza, spaghetti, and garlic bread.

Steve was senior pastor of a church of between fifteen hundred and two thousand people—nearly as many people as lived in our hometown of Imperial. It was a chance for Sonja and me to get to know another pastor in our district and to get some ideas on how other pastors do ministry. We planned to visit Steve's church, Greeley Wesleyan, the next day. Sonja especially wanted to get a look at how the church's Sunday morning children's program worked. Rebecca divided her time between the grown-up conversation and coloring with the kids.

"Wow, Colton, you're doing a really good job coloring that pizza!" she said. Colton offered a thin, polite smile but had fallen unusually quiet. Then, a few minutes later, he said, "Mommy, my tummy hurts."

Sonja and I exchanged a glance. Was it the stomach flu coming back? Sonja laid the back of her hand against Colton's cheek and shook her head. "You don't feel hot, hon."

"I think I'm gonna throw up," Colton said.

"I don't feel so good, either, Mommy," Cassie said.

We figured it was something they ate. With both kids feeling under the weather, we ended our dinner early, said good-bye to the Wilsons, and headed back to the hotel, which was just across the parking lot from the restaurant. As soon as we got the door to our room open, Colton's prediction came true: he upchucked, beginning on the carpet and ending, as Sonja whisked him into the tiny bathroom, in the toilet.

Standing in the bathroom doorway, I watched Colton's small form bent over and convulsing. This didn't seem like any kind of food poisoning.

Gotta be that stomach flu, I thought. *Great.*

That was how the evening began. It continued with Colton throwing up every thirty minutes like clockwork. Between times, Sonja sat in an upholstered side chair with Colton on her lap, keeping the room's ice bucket within reach in case she couldn't make it to the bathroom. About two hours into this cycle, another kid joined the party. As Colton was in the bathroom, heaving into the toilet with Sonja kneeling beside him, a steadying hand on his back, Cassie ran in and threw up in the tub.

"Todd!" Sonja called. "I need a little help in here!"

Great, I thought. *Now they both have it.*

Or did they? After we were able to move both kids back to the bedroom, Sonja and I put our heads together. Colton had seemed to kick that stomach flu the day before. And all day long at the Butterfly Pavilion, he was his normal self, completely happy except for the strain of holding Rosie to get that sticker. Cassie had held Rosie too . . . could Goliath tarantulas trigger a case of double upchuck?

No, dummy, I told myself and pushed the thought aside.

"Did the kids eat the same thing at the restaurant?" I asked Sonja, who by then was lying on one of the double beds with one arm around each of our two green-at-the-gills kids.

She looked at the ceiling and thought for a moment. "I think they both had some pizza . . . but we all had pizza. I think it's that flu. Colton probably wasn't over it quite yet, and he passed it along to Cassie before we got here. The doctor said it was pretty contagious."

No matter what, it looked like our relaxing, post-turmoil celebration trip was abruptly coming to an end. And a few minutes later, I heard the magic words that seemed to confirm my thoughts: "Mommy, I feel like I'm gonna throw up again."

Sonja snatched up Colton and hustled him to the toilet again, just in the nick of time.

When the pink light of dawn began peeking through the curtains the next morning, Sonja was still awake. We had agreed that at least one of us should still go visit Greeley Wesleyan and get some large-church ministry knowledge we could export to Imperial, so I tried to get at least a little sleep. That left Sonja with nursing duties, which included an almost hourly trek back and forth to the bathroom with Colton. Cassie had gotten sick only one other time during the night, but whatever this bug was, it seemed to have latched onto our little boy's innards and dug in deep.

We checked out of the hotel early and drove over to the Greeley home of Phil and Betty Lou Harris, our close friends and also superintendents for the Wesleyan church district that includes all of Colorado and Nebraska. The original plan had been that our two families would attend the Wilsons' church together that morning. Now, though, with a pair of sick kids, we decided that Sonja would stay at the Harrises' home. Betty Lou, sweet lady that she is, volunteered to stay home and assist.

When I got back from church just after lunch, Sonja gave me the status report: Cassie was feeling a lot better. She had even been able to eat a little something and keep it down. But Colton continued to vomit on a clockwork basis and had been unable to hold anything down.

Colton was in the Harrises' living room, huddled in the corner of the huge couch on top of a blanket/drop cloth with a bucket standing nearby just in case. I walked over and sat down beside him.

"Hey, buddy. Not doing so great, huh?"

Colton slowly shook his head, and tears welled up in his blue eyes. I might've been in my thirties, but over the last few months, I'd learned only too well what it was like to feel so sick and miserable that you just wanted to cry. My heart hurt for my son.

"Come here," I said. I pulled him into my lap and looked into his little round face. His eyes, usually sparkling and playful, looked flat and weak.

Phil walked over and sat down beside me and reviewed the symptoms: abdominal pain, profuse vomiting, a fever that had come and gone. "Could it be appendicitis?"

I thought about it for a moment. There was certainly a family history. My uncle's appendix had burst, and I'd had a wicked case of appendicitis in college during the time Sonja and I were dating. Also, Sonja had had her appendix out when she was in second grade.

But the circumstances here didn't seem to fit the bill. The doctor in Imperial had diagnosed him with stomach flu. And if it was appendicitis, there would be no reason Cassie would be sick too.

We spent Sunday night with the Harrises in Greeley. By morning, Cassie had completely recovered, but Colton had spent a second night throwing up.

As we packed our duffel bags and headed outside to load up the Expedition, Phil gazed at Colton, cradled in Sonja's arms. "He looks pretty sick to me, Todd. Maybe you should take him to the hospital here."

Sonja and I had discussed that option. We had sat in emergency room waiting areas with a sick kid before, and our experience was that we could probably make the three-hour drive back to Imperial before we would be seen in the emergency room of a metro-Denver hospital. So instead, we called ahead to Imperial and made an appointment with our regular family doctor, the one Colton had seen the previous

Friday. I explained our reasoning to Phil. He said he understood, but I could tell he was still worried. And by the time we'd been on the road for an hour or so, I began to think that maybe he had been right.

For Sonja, our first red flag waved when we stopped at a Safeway just outside Greeley to buy Pull-Ups. Colton, who had been potty-trained for more than two years, had tinkled in his underwear. It worried Sonja that he didn't even protest when she laid him down in the backseat of the Expedition and helped him into a pair of Pull-Ups. Under normal circumstances, he would have been indignant: "I'm not a *baby!*" Now, though, he didn't utter a peep.

Instead, once strapped back into his car seat, he only clutched his belly and moaned. Two hours into the drive, he was crying constantly, stopping about every thirty minutes to throw up again. In the rearview mirror, I could see the heartbreak and helplessness on Sonja's face. Meanwhile, I tried to focus on the goal: get him to Imperial, get some IVs in him, stop the dehydration that surely must be setting in as this flu ran its course.

We reached Imperial in just under three hours. At the hospital, a nurse took us back to an examination room pretty quickly, with Sonja carrying Colton, cradling his head against her shoulder the way she had when he was an infant. Within a few minutes, the doctor who had seen Colton on Friday joined us, and we brought him up to date on the situation. After a brief exam, he ordered blood tests and an Xray, and I think I took a breath for the first time since we rolled out of Greeley. This was progress. We were doing something. In a short while, we'd have a diagnosis, probably a prescription or two, and Colton would be on the way to recovery.

We took Colton to the lab, where he screamed as a tech tried her best to find a vein. That was followed by Xrays that were better only because we convinced Colton that there were no needles involved. Within an hour, we were back in the exam room with the doctor.

"Could it be appendicitis?" Sonja asked the doctor.

He shook his head. "No. Colton's white blood cell count isn't consistent with appendicitis. We are concerned, though, about his Xrays."

I looked at Sonja. It was at that moment we realized we'd been banking on a really nasty virus. We were completely unprepared for something more serious. The doctor led us into the hallway, where there was already an Xray clipped to an illuminator. When I saw what was in the picture, my heart dropped into my stomach: The Xray of our son's tiny little torso showed three dark masses. It looked for all the world as if his insides had exploded.

Sonja began shaking her head and tears, which had hovered just beneath the surface, spilled onto her cheeks.

"Are you sure it's not appendicitis?" I asked the doctor. "There's a family history."

Again he said no. "That's not what the blood tests show."

"Then what is it?"

"I'm not sure," he said.

FIVE

SHADOW OF DEATH

That was Monday, March 3. Nurses placed Colton in a room and inserted an IV. Two bags dangled from the top of a stainless steel pole, one for hydration and one with antibiotics of some kind. Sonja and I prayed together for Colton. Norma stopped by with Colton's favorite toy, his Spider-Man action figure. Normally, his eyes would've lit up at the sight of either Norma *or* Spider-Man, but Colton didn't react at all. Later, our friend Terri brought Colton's best little buddy, her son Hunter, to visit. Again, Colton was unresponsive, almost lifeless.

Sitting in a side chair near Colton's bed, Norma looked at Sonja grimly. "I think you should take him to Children's Hospital in Denver."

But at that point, we were trusting in the doctors, confident that everything was being done that could be done. Besides, Colton was in no condition to travel all the way back to Colorado.

Colton continued to throw up. Sonja held down the fort, comforting him, catching his vomit, while I drove home to check in on the rest of our lives. On the way, I stopped by the church to make sure the place hadn't burned down. I checked in with my garage-door guys, returned some phone calls from new customers, and went out to do a door repair job. The entire time I was away from the hospital, I sent up prayers. Even during my conversations with others, my prayers ascended, a kind of mental background music that would've been in the foreground—the only ground—if only life didn't have an annoying way of rolling on.

Sonja spent Monday night at the hospital, and I stayed home with Cassie. On Tuesday morning, I took her to school. During the rest of the day, between church and company responsibilities, I popped in and out of the hospital as often as I could, hoping for some improvement. Instead, each time I walked into Colton's room, I saw my little boy slipping deeper into the grip of whatever mysterious monster held him. Not only was he not getting better; he was getting worse *faster*.

By the second afternoon, I saw something that terrified me: the shadow of death.

I recognized it instantly. As a pastor, you sometimes find yourself on a deathwatch. In a hospital. A nursing home. A hospice. There are telltale signs: the skin loses its pinkness and fades to a jaundiced yellow. Breathing is labored. The eyes are open but the person is not present. And most telling of all, a sinking and darkening around the eyes. I had seen this look many times, but in a context where you might expect it, in a patient suffering from terminal cancer or in the final phases of old age. You know that person's life on earth has come down to days, then hours, then minutes. I would be there to comfort the family, to pray with them prayers like, *God, please take her soon. Please take away her pain.*

This time, though, I was seeing the shadow of death again—and I was seeing it on my son. My not-quite-four-year-old son. The sight hit me like a bullet.

A voice screamed inside my head, *We're not doing anything!*

I'm a pacer. I wore ruts in the floor of Colton's room, crossing the tiny space again and again like a caged lion. My stomach churned. Inside my chest, an invisible vise squeezed my heart. *He's getting worse, God! What do we do?*

While I paced, Sonja channeled her anxiety into the role of busy caretaker. She fluffed Colton's pillow, arranged his blankets, made sure he was still drinking. It was a role she was filling to keep from exploding. Each time I looked at her, I could see the agitation growing in her eyes. Our son was slipping away and, like me, she wanted to know: What. Was. Wrong? The doctors would bring back test results, test results, test results. But no answers, only useless observations. "He doesn't seem to be responding to the medication. I don't know . . . I wish the surgeon was here."

Sonja and I wrestled with trust. We weren't doctors. We had no medical experience. I'm a pastor; she's a teacher. We wanted to trust. We wanted to believe the medical professionals were doing everything that could be done. We kept thinking, *Next time the doctor walks in, he'll have new test results; he'll change the medication; he'll do something to get that look of death off our son.*

But he didn't. And there came a point when we had to draw the line.

SIX

NORTH PLATTE

On Wednesday, we broke the news to the Imperial hospital staff that we were taking Colton to the Great Plains Regional Medical Center in North Platte. We considered Norma's suggestion of Children's in Denver, but felt it would be better to stay closer to our base of support. It took a while to get Colton checked out, as it does anytime you leave a hospital, but to us it seemed an eternity. Finally, a nurse came in with the discharge papers, a copy of Colton's test results, and a large, flat brown envelope containing his Xrays. Sonja called ahead to the office of pediatrician Dr. Dell Shepherd to let his staff know we were coming.

At 10:30 a.m., I picked Colton up out of the hospital bed and was shocked at the limpness of his body. He felt like a rag in my arms. It would've been a great time to panic, but I tried to keep my cool. At least we were doing something now. We were taking action.

Colton's car seat was strapped into the backseat of our SUV. Gently, I laid him in, wondering as I buckled him in how fast I could make the ninety-minute trip to North Platte. Sonja climbed into the backseat with Colton, armed with a pink plastic hospital dish for catching vomit.

The day was sunny but cold. As I steered the SUV onto Highway 61, I twisted the rearview mirror so that I could see Colton. Several miles passed in silence; then I heard him retching into the bowl. When he was finished, I pulled over so that Sonja could empty it onto the side of the road. Back on the highway, I glanced in the mirror and saw Sonja slip the Xray film from the brown envelope and hold it up in the streaming sunlight. Slowly, she began shaking her head, and tears filled her eyes.

"We screwed up," she said, her voice breaking over the images she would later tell me were burned in her mind forever.

I turned my head back enough to see the three small explosions she was staring at. The misshapen blotches seemed huge in the ghostly image of Colton's tiny torso. Why did they seem so much bigger now?

"You're right. We should've known," I said.

"But the doctor . . ."

"I know. We shouldn't have listened."

There wasn't any finger-pointing, no blaming each other. But we were both really upset with ourselves. We had tried to do the right thing at each step. The doctor said Xrays; we did Xrays. The doctor said IVs; we did IVs. The doctor said blood tests; we did blood tests. He was the doctor, right? He knew what he was doing . . . right? At each turning point, we had tried to make the right call, but we had made the wrong ones, and now Colton was paying for it. A helpless child was suffering the consequences of our mistakes.

Behind me, Colton slumped lifelessly in his car seat, and his silence was louder than any sound I had ever heard.

There is a story in the Bible about King David of Israel. David had committed adultery with Bathsheba, the wife of Uriah, one of David's trusted soldiers. Then, in an effort to cover up his sin, David sent Uriah to the front lines, where David knew he would be killed. Later, the prophet Nathan came to David and said, basically, "Look, God knows what you did, and here are the consequences of your sin: the child that you and Bathsheba have conceived will not live."[1]

David tore his clothes and cried and prayed and pleaded with God. He was so grief-stricken that when the baby died, his servants were afraid to come and tell him. But David figured it out, and when he did, he got up, washed himself, ate, and calmly took care of the funeral. His behavior confused his servants, who said, "Hey, wait a minute: weren't you just freaking out a few minutes ago? Weren't you just pleading and crying before God? Now you're so calm . . . what's the deal?"

David explained, "I was hoping God would change his mind. But he didn't."[2]

In his mind, David had been doing what he could while there was still something he could do.

When I think back on that drive to North Platte, that's how I felt. Yes, the X-rays looked bad, and my son's face was covered in death.

But he wasn't dead yet.

Now was not the time to quit and mourn. Now was the time for prayer and action. *God, let us get there. Let us help our son.*

As a father, I felt I had blown it. But maybe there was still something I could do to redeem myself. That hope was probably the only thing that kept me from falling apart.

We crossed the North Platte line at about noon and made a beeline for the pediatrician's office. I hustled out of the SUV and bundled Colton in a blanket, carrying him in my arms like a fireman. Sonja gathered up our gear and followed me in, still carrying the hospital bowl.

At the reception desk, a pleasant woman greeted us.

"We're the Burpos," I said. "We called ahead from Imperial about our son."

"The doctor has gone to lunch."

Gone to lunch?!

"But we called ahead," I said. "He knew we were coming."

"Please have a seat," the receptionist said. "The doctor will be back in ten or fifteen minutes."

Her routine manner told me she did not feel our urgency, and inside me, a rocket of anger went off. On the outside, though, I kept my cool. I could've screamed and hollered, but it wouldn't have done any good. Also, I'm a pastor. We don't have the luxury of publicly losing it.

Sonja and I found a seat in the waiting area, and fifteen minutes later, the doctor arrived. He had the soothing appearance of maturity—silver hair, glasses, a trim moustache. The nursing staff ushered us back to an exam room, and Sonja handed him the packet of tests we'd brought, along with the

Xrays. He examined Colton so briefly that it occurred to me
he might be making up for lost time.

"I'm going to order a CT scan," he said. "You'll need to
head across the street to the hospital."

He meant the Great Plains Regional Medical Center.
Ten minutes later, we found ourselves in the imaging clinic
in perhaps the most important argument of our lives.

SEVEN

"I THINK THIS IS IT"

"Noooo!"

"But Colton, you *have* to drink it!"

"Noooo! It's yuh-keeeee!"

Colton's screams of protest echoed through the clinic. He was so exhausted, so frail, so tired of throwing up his guts, and now we were trying to make him drink a thick, gritty, cherry-red solution that a sane adult wouldn't drink voluntarily in a million years. Finally, Colton took a little sip, but then immediately heaved it up again. Sonja swooped in to catch it in the bowl.

"He's throwing up all the time," I told the imaging technician. "How's he going to drink it?"

"I'm sorry, sir . . . he has to drink it so we can get the best images."

"Ple-e-ease! Please don't make me drink it, Daddy!"

We tried everything. We played good cop/bad cop, Sonja coaxing while I threatened. But the firmer I got, the more

Colton clamped his teeth together and refused the sticky liquid.

I tried reasoning: "Colton, if you can just get this down, the doctors can do this test and we can get you feeling better. Don't you want to feel better?"

Sniffles. "Yeah."

"Well, here then, take a drink."

"*Noooooo! Don't make meeee!*"

We were desperate. If he didn't drink the fluid, they couldn't do the CT scan. Without the CT scan, they couldn't diagnose. Without a diagnosis, they couldn't treat our son. The battle raged for nearly an hour until, finally, a technician came out and had mercy on us. "Let's go ahead and take him in. We'll just do the best we can."

Inside the imaging room, Sonja stood with the tech behind the radiation shield while I stood beside a listless Colton as the moving table slid him into a big, scary tube. Showing tenderness and compassion, the tech stopped the table before it slid Colton fully into the machine, allowing him to keep his head out so that he could see me. The machine whirred to life, and Colton stared at me through eyes pinched with pain.

Just like that, the test was over. The technician scanned the pictures, then escorted us out of the lab. He did not take us back to the main waiting room, but to an isolated hallway where a few chairs lined the wall.

The technician looked at me somberly. "You need to wait here," he said. At the time, I didn't even notice that he had not asked Colton to get dressed.

The three of us sat in the cold, narrow hallway, Sonja cradling Colton, his head against her shoulder. She was crying pretty steadily now. Looking in her eyes, I could see that her hope had drained away. This wasn't the normal place where you would wait. The tech had separated us out. He had seen the picture and knew it was something bad.

Sonja looked down at Colton, lying in her arms, and I could see the wheels turning in her head. She and Colton did *everything* together. This was her little boy, her pal. More than that, this little blond-haired, blue-eyed fireball was a heavenly blessing, a healing gift after the baby we had lost.

Five years earlier, Sonja had been pregnant with our second child. We were over the moon about it, seeing this new life as the rounding out of our family. When it was just the two of us, we were a couple. When Cassie was born, we became a family. With a second child on the way, we could begin to see the outlines of the future—family portraits, a house filled with the joyful noise of childhood, two kids checking their stockings on Christmas morning. Then two months into the pregnancy, Sonja lost the baby, and our misty-edged dreams popped like soap bubbles. Grief consumed Sonja. The reality of a child lost, one we would never know. An empty space where there wasn't one before.

We were eager to try again, but we worried about whether we would be able to have another child, multiplying our misery. A few months later, Sonja became pregnant again. Her early prenatal checkups revealed a healthy, growing baby. Still, we hung on a bit loosely, a little afraid to fall in love with this new child as we had the one we had lost. But forty weeks later, on May 19, 1999, Colton Todd Burpo arrived and we fell head over heels. For Sonja, this little boy was an even more special gift directly from the hand of a loving, heavenly Father.

Now, as I watched her face above Colton's pale form, I could see terrible questions forming in her mind: *What are you doing, God? Are you going to take this child too?*

Colton's face appeared pinched and pale, his face a tiny moon in the stark hallway. The shadows around his eyes had deepened into dark, purple hollows. He wasn't screaming anymore, or even crying. He was just . . . still.

Again it reminded me of those dying patients I had seen hovering on the threshold between earth and eternity. Tears filled my eyes, blurring the image of my son like rain on a windowpane. Sonja looked up at me, her own tears streaming. "I think this is it," she said.

EIGHT

RAGING AT GOD

Five minutes later, a white-coated man emerged from the imaging lab. I don't remember his name, but I remember that his name tag said "Radiologist."

"Your son has a ruptured appendix," he said. "He needs emergency surgery. They're ready for you in surgical prep now. Follow me."

Astonished, Sonja and I fell in behind him. Heat surged in my temples. *A burst appendix?* Hadn't the doctor in Imperial ruled that out?

In the surgical prep room, Sonja laid Colton on a gurney, kissed his forehead, and stepped away as a nurse closed in with an IV bag and a needle. Immediately, Colton began to scream and thrash. I stood at my son's head and held his shoulders down, trying to soothe him with my voice. Sonja returned to Colton's side, crying openly as she kept trying to brace his left arm and leg with her body.

When I looked up, the prep room was crowded with men and women in white coats and scrubs. "The surgeon is here," one of them said, gently. "If you'll step out and talk with him, we'll take over in here."

Reluctantly, we stepped through the curtain, Colton screaming, *"Pleeease, Daddy! Don't go!"*

In the hallway, Dr. Timothy O'Holleran waited for us. Dr. O'Holleran was the doctor who had performed the lumpectomy on me four months earlier. Now his features were set in grim horizontal lines.

He didn't waste words. "Colton's appendix has ruptured. He's not in good shape. We're going to go in and try to clean him out."

On the other side of the curtain, Colton was still screaming. *"Daddy! Daaadd-eeee!"*

Gritting my teeth, I shut out the sound and tried to focus on the doctor.

"We asked about a burst appendix in Imperial," Sonja said. "They ruled it out."

My brain skipped over the past and looked toward the future, angling for hope. "How do you think he'll do?" I said.

"We've got to go in and clean him out. We'll know more when we open him up."

The spaces between his words rang in my ears like alarm bells as Colton's screams rang down the halls. In response to a direct question, the doctor had specifically *not* given us any assurances. In fact, the only thing he had said about Colton was that he was in bad shape. My mind flashed back to the moment Sonja called me in Greeley from Imperial to tell me Colton's fever had broken, and that they were on their way. What had seemed like the end of a stomach flu had more likely been the first sign of a ruptured appendix. That meant poison had been filling our little boy's belly for *five days*. That tally explained the shadow of death we saw on him now. And it explained why Dr. O'Holleran had not offered us any hope.

The doctor nodded toward the noise spilling from the prep room. "I think it'll work better if we take him back to surgery and sedate him, then put in the IV."

He stepped over to the curtain and I heard him give the order. A few moments later, two nurses wheeled the gurney through the curtain, and I saw Colton writhing. He twisted his tiny form, turning his head until he locked onto me with his sunken eyes. *"Daddy! Don't let them take meeee!"*

Remember when I said pastors don't have the luxury of losing it? I was about to lose it, and I had to get away. After talking to the doctor and then scribbling my name on what seemed to be hundreds of insurance forms, nearly running, I found a small room with a door, ducked in, and slammed it shut behind me. My heart raced. I couldn't get my breath. Desperation, anger, and frustration washed over me in waves that seemed to squeeze away my breath.

When everybody's freaking out, they all look to Dad—especially when Dad's a pastor. Now I was finally in a room where no one was looking at me, and I began raging at God.

"Where *are* you? Is *this* how you treat your pastors?! Is it even worth it to serve you?"

Back and forth, I paced the room, which seemed to close in on me, shrinking as surely as Colton's options were shrinking. Over and over a single image assaulted me: Colton being wheeled away, his arms stretched out, screaming for me to save him.

That's when it hit me. *We waited too long. I might never see my son alive again.*

Tears of rage flooded my eyes, spilled onto my cheeks. "After the leg, the kidney stones, the lumpectomy, *this* is how you're going to let me celebrate the end of my time of testing?" I yelled at God. "You're going to take my son?"

NINE

MINUTES LIKE GLACIERS

Fifteen minutes later, maybe more, I emerged from that room dry-eyed. It had been the first time I'd really been alone since the whole ordeal began. I had wanted to be strong for Sonja, a husband strong for his wife. I found her in the waiting room, using her last drops of cell phone battery to call friends and family. I hugged her and held her as she cried into my shirt until it stuck to my chest. I used what little battery was left on my cell phone to call Terri, my secretary, who would in turn activate the prayer chain at church. This was not a ritual call. I was desperate for prayer, desperate that other believers would bang on the gates of heaven and beg for the life of our son.

Pastors are supposed to be unshakable pillars of faith, right? But at that moment, my faith was hanging by a tattered thread and fraying fast. I thought of the times where the Scripture says that God answered the prayers, not of the sick or dying, but of the *friends* of the sick or dying—the paralytic, for example. It was when Jesus saw the faith of the man's friends that he told the paralytic, "Get up, take your mat and go home."[1] At that moment, I needed to borrow the strength and faith of some other believers. After I hung up with Terri, Sonja and I sat together and prayed, afraid to hope and afraid not to.

Time dragged, the minutes moving at the speed of glaciers. Between muted conversations and small talk, the waiting room ticked with a pregnant silence.

Ninety minutes later, a female nurse in purple scrubs, a surgical mask dangling from her neck, stepped into the waiting room. "Is Colton's father here?"

The tone of her voice, and the fact that it was a nurse and not Dr. O'Holleran, sent a surge of hope through my body.

Maybe God is being gracious despite our stupidity. Maybe he's going to give us another day, another chance.

I stood. "I'm Colton's dad."

"Mr. Burpo, can you come back? Colton's out of surgery, but we can't calm him down. He's still screaming, and he's screaming for you."

When they were wheeling Colton away, I couldn't bear his screams. Now, suddenly, I wanted to hear his screams more than I'd ever wanted to hear anything in my life. To me, they would be a beautiful sound.

Sonja and I gathered up our things and followed the nurse back through the wide double doors that led to the surgical ward. We didn't make it to the recovery room but met a pair of nurses wheeling Colton through the hallway on a gurney. He was alert, and I could tell he'd been looking for me. My first reaction was to try to get as close as I could to him; I think I would've climbed on the gurney with him if I hadn't thought the nurses might feel a little put out.

The nurses stopped long enough for Sonja and I each to plant a kiss on Colton's little face, which still looked pale and drawn. "Hey, buddy, how you doin'?" I said.

"Hi, Mommy. Hi, Daddy." The ghost of a smile warmed his face.

The nurses got the gurney under way again, and a few minutes and an elevator ride later, Colton was settled into a narrow hospital room at the end of a long corridor. Sonja stepped out of the room for a moment to take care of some paperwork at the nurse's station, and I stayed behind, sitting next to Colton's bed in one of those mesh-covered rockers, drinking in my son's aliveness.

A small child looks even smaller in a hospital bed built for grown-ups. At under forty pounds, Colton's body barely raised the sheet. His feet reached no more than a third of the way down the bed. Dark rings still circled his eyes, but it seemed to me that the blue of his eyes shone brighter than two hours before.

"Daddy?" Colton looked at me earnestly.

"What?"

He gazed at me and didn't move his eyes from mine.

"Daddy, you know I almost died."

Fear gripped me. *Where did he hear that?*

Had he overheard the medical staff talking? Had he heard something the surgical team said, despite the anesthesia? Because we certainly hadn't said anything about his being close to death in front of him. Sonja and I had feared he was at the brink, had *known* it after we learned his appendix had been leaking poison into his system for five days. But we'd been very careful not to say anything in front of Colton that would scare him.

My throat closed, the first sign of tears. Some people freak out when their teenagers want to talk about sex. If you think that's tough, try talking to your preschooler about dying. Colton had been with me in nursing homes, places where people gave their loved ones permission to let go of life. I wasn't about to give my son permission to quit. We weren't out of the woods yet, and I didn't want him to think that death was an option.

I willed my voice to remain steady and smiled at my son. "You just think about getting better, okay, buddy?"

"Okay, Daddy."

"We're here with you all the way. We're praying for you." I changed the subject. "Now, what can we bring you? Do you want your action figures from home?"

We hadn't been in the room long when three members of our church board arrived at the hospital. We were so grateful for that. Sometimes I wonder, what do people do when they have no extended family and no church? In times of crisis, where does their support come from? Cassie stayed with Norma and Bryan in Imperial until my mother, Kay, could drive up from Ulysses, Kansas. Bryan's extended family lives in North Platte, and they came to help us too. Our church gathering around us in the eye of the storm would change the way Sonja and I approached pastoral visitation in times of trial and grief. We were faithful about it before; now we're militant.

Soon, Sonja came back into the room and not long after that, Dr. O'Holleran joined us. Colton lay quietly as the surgeon pulled back the sheet to show us the incision site, a horizontal line across the right side of his tiny belly. The wound was packed with blood-tinged gauze, and as he began to remove it, Colton whimpered a bit in fear. I don't think he could feel it yet, since he was still under the effects of the local anesthesia the surgical team had applied to the incision site.

Colton's insides were so contaminated with the poison of the ruptured appendix that Dr. O'Holleran had decided it was best to leave his incision open so it could continue to drain.

Now the doctor spread the wound slightly.

"See that gray tissue?" he said. "That's what happens to internal organs when there's an infection. Colton's not going to be able to leave the hospital until everything that's gray in there turns pink."

A length of plastic tubing protruded from each side of Colton's abdomen. At the end of each tube was what the doctor called a "grenade." Clear plastic in color, they did look a little like grenades, but they were actually manual squeeze pumps. The next morning, Dr. O'Holleran showed us how to squeeze the grenades to drain pus from Colton's abdomen and then pack the opening with fresh gauze. For the next few days, Dr. O'Holleran would arrive each morning to check the wound and pack the dressing. Colton screamed bloody murder during those visits and began to associate the doctor with everything bad that was happening to him.

In the evenings, when the doctor wasn't there, I had to drain the incision. Prior to the surgery, Sonja had been on puke patrol for nearly a week and since the surgery, at Colton's bedside every minute. But draining the pus was gory work and, for her, a bridge too far. Besides, it took at least three adults to hold Colton down. So while I squeezed the grenades, Sonja helped two nurses hold him, Sonja whispering soothing words while Colton screamed and screamed.

PRAYERS OF A
MOST UNUSUAL KIND

For another week after the emergency appendectomy, Colton continued to throw up, and we continued to pump poison out of his body twice a day using Dr. O'Holleran's rigging of plastic tubing and grenades. Slowly, gradually, Colton took a turn for the better. The upchucking stopped, his color returned, and he began to eat a little. We knew he was on the mend when he began to sit up and chat with us, play with the video game console the nurses had stationed at his bed, and even take an interest in the brand-new stuffed lion that Cassie had brought him several days before. Finally, seven days after we checked in to the hospital in North Platte, the medical team said we could take our son home.

Like soldiers after a long but victorious fight, Sonja and I were both exhausted and overjoyed. On March 13, we packed up all the debris of a lengthy hospital stay in a hodgepodge of shopping bags, duffel bags, and plastic bags and headed for the elevators, me pushing Colton in a wheelchair and Sonja holding a thick bouquet of going-home balloons.

The elevator doors had begun sliding shut when Dr. O'Holleran appeared in the hallway and literally yelled for us to stop. "You can't go! You can't go!" His voice echoed in the tile corridor as he waved a sheaf of paper in our direction. "We've still got problems!"

A last-minute blood test had revealed a radical spike in Colton's white cell count, Dr. O'Holleran told us when he caught up to us at the elevator. "It's probably another abscess," he said. "We may have to operate again."

I thought Sonja was going to pass out right there. Both of us were walking zombies by then and had nearly reached our limit. Colton burst into tears.

Another CT scan revealed new pockets of infection in Colton's abdomen. That afternoon, Dr. O'Holleran and his surgical team had to open up our little boy a second time and clean him out again. This time, Sonja and I weren't terrified; the shadow of death had long since passed from Colton's face. But now we had a new worry: Colton hadn't eaten for something like ten days. He had weighed only about forty pounds to begin with, and now he had melted away so that his elbows and knees appeared abnormally large, his face thin like a hungry orphan.

After the surgery, I brought our concerns to Dr. O'Holleran. "He hasn't eaten more than a little Jell-O or broth in almost two weeks," I said. "How long can a kid go without eating?"

Dr. O'Holleran placed Colton in the intensive care unit and ordered extra nutrition for him, administered through a feeding tube. But the ICU bed was as much for us as for Colton, I suspect. We hadn't slept for nearly as long as Colton hadn't eaten, and we were absolutely ragged. Putting Colton in ICU was the only way the doctor could get us to go get some rest.

"Colton will be fine tonight," he told us. "He'll have his own nurse at all times, and if anything happens, someone will be right there to take care of him."

I have to admit, those words sounded like an oasis in a desert of exhaustion.

We were afraid to leave Colton alone, but we knew Dr. O'Holleran was right. That night was the first night since leaving the Harrises' home in Greeley that Sonja and I spent together. We talked. We cried. We encouraged each other. But mostly, we slept like shipwreck survivors on their first warm, dry night.

After a night in the ICU, Colton was moved to yet another hospital room, and the wait-and-see cycle began all over again. *When can Colton get out of here? When can we go home and be normal again?* Now, though, Colton's bowels seemed to have stopped working. He couldn't use the bathroom, and hour by hour, he grew more miserable.

"Daddy, my tummy hurts," he moaned, lying in bed. The doctor said that even if Colton could pass gas, that would be a good sign. We tried walking him up and down the halls to shake things loose, but Colton could only shuffle along slowly, hunched over in pain. Nothing seemed to help. By the fourth day after the second surgery, he could only lie on the bed, writhing as constipation set in. That afternoon, Dr. O'Holleran came with more bad news.

"I'm sorry," he said. "I know you've been through a lot, but I think we've done everything for Colton we can do here. We're thinking maybe it would be best to transfer him to a children's hospital. Either the one in Omaha or the one in Denver."

Between us, we'd managed something like five nights' sleep in fifteen days. After more than two grueling weeks at Colton's bedside, we had nearly hit the road back to normal—with the elevator doors literally closing, our family inside with balloons—when the whole thing crashed around us again. And now, our son was back in excruciating pain with no end in sight. We couldn't even see a horizon.

Just when we thought it couldn't get any worse, it did: a freak spring snowstorm was moving into the Midwest. Within a couple of hours, thick drifts of snow lay piled against the hospital doors and wheel-well high in the parking lots. Whether we chose the children's hospital in Omaha, eight hours away, or Denver, three hours away, there would be no way short of an airlift that we could reach either one.

That's when Sonja lost it. "I can't do this anymore!" she said and broke down in tears.

And right about then was when a group of people in our church decided it was time for some serious prayer. Church friends began making phone calls, and before long, around eighty people had driven over to Crossroads Wesleyan for a prayer service. Some were in our congregation and some from other churches, but they had all come together to pray for our son.

Brad Dillan called me on my cell to tell me what was going on. "What, specifically, can we pray for?" he asked.

Feeling a little odd about it, I told him what Dr. O'Holleran had said would be a good sign for Colton. So that night might be the only time in recorded history that eighty people gathered and prayed for someone to pass gas!

Of course, they also prayed for a break in the weather so that we could get to Denver, and they prayed for healing too. But within an hour, the first prayer was answered!

Immediately, Colton began to feel better. That evening, he was able to use the bathroom. By the next morning, he was up in his room, playing as though none of this nightmare had ever happened. Watching him, Sonja and I couldn't believe our eyes: except for being skinny, Colton was completely and utterly himself again. In less than twelve hours, we had cycled from completely desperate to completely normal.

Around 9 a.m., Dr. O'Holleran came in to check on his patient. When he saw Colton up, smiling and chipper, and playing with his action figures, the doctor was speechless. For a long moment, he actually just stood and stared. Astonished, he examined Colton and then scheduled another round of tests to be triple-sure that Colton's insides were on the mend. This time, Colton literally skipped all the way to the CT scan lab.

We stayed in the hospital another day and a half just to be certain Colton's turnaround stuck. During those thirty-six hours, it seemed we had more nurses in and out than usual. Slowly, one at a time and in pairs, they would slip into the room—and each time, their reaction was the same: they just stood and stared at our little boy.

ELEVEN

COLTON BURPO, COLLECTION AGENT

After we got home from the hospital, we slept for a week. Okay, I'm exaggerating—but not much. Sonja and I were completely drained. It was like we had just been through a seventeen-day almost-car-crash. Our wounds weren't visible on the outside, but the soul-tearing worry and tension had taken its toll.

One evening about a week after we got home, Sonja and I were standing in the kitchen talking about money. She stood over a portable table next to our microwave, sorting through the enormous stack of mail that had accumulated during Colton's hospital stay. Each time she opened an envelope, she jotted down a number on a sheet of paper lying on the counter. Even from where I stood leaning against the cabinets on the opposite side of the kitchen, I could see that the column of figures was getting awfully long.

Finally, she clicked the pen closed and laid it on the

counter. "Do you know how much money I need to pay the bills this week?"

As both the family and business bookkeeper, Sonja asked me that question regularly. She worked part-time as a teacher so we had that steady income, but it was a relatively small stream. My pastor's salary was also small, cobbled together from the tithes of a small but faithful congregation. So the bulk of the earning came from our garage-door business, and that income waxed and waned with the seasons. Every couple of weeks, she presented me with the figures—not only on household bills but on business payables. Now there were also several massive hospital bills.

I performed a rough tally in my head and offered her a guess. "Probably close to $23,000, right?"

"Yep," she said, and sighed.

It might as well have been a million bucks. With me unable to work the garage-door jobs because of my broken leg and then the hyperplasia, we had already burned through our savings. Then, just when I was getting back into full swing, Colton's illness hit, knocking me out of work for nearly another month. We had about as much chance of coming up with $23,000 as we did of winning the lottery. And since we don't play the lottery, those chances were zero.

"Do you have any receivables? Anything due you can collect?" Sonja said.

She asked because she had to, but she knew the answer. I shook my head.

"I can put off some of these," she said, nodding toward the envelope stack. "But the tenth bills are definitely due."

Here's a great picture of how small a town Imperial actually is: folks have tabs or accounts they run at places like the gas station, the grocery store, and the hardware store. So if we need a fill-up or a loaf of bread, we just swing by and sign for it. Then on the tenth of the month, Sonja makes a fifteen-minute trip around town to settle up. Our "tenth bills" are one of the cool things about living in a small town. On the other hand, when you can't pay, it's a lot more humbling.

I sighed. "I can go explain the situation, ask for more time."

Sonja held up a sheaf of papers a little thicker than the others. "The medical bills are starting to come in. One of them is $34,000."

"How much will the insurance cover?"

"There's a $3,200 deductible."

"We can't even pay that right now," I said.

"Do you still want me to write the tithe check?" Sonja asked, referring to our regular weekly donation to the church.

"Absolutely," I said. God had just given us our son back; there was no way we were not going to give back to God.

At just that moment, Colton came around the corner from the living room and surprised us with a strange proclamation that I can still hear to this day.

He stood at the end of the counter with his hands on his hips. "Dad, Jesus used Dr. O'Holleran to fix me," he said. His preschool face was oddly self-assured. "You need to pay him."

Then he turned around and marched out. Around the corner and gone.

Sonja and I looked at each other. *What?*

We were both a little taken aback, since Colton had seen the surgeon as the source of all the poking, cutting, prodding, draining, and pain. Now here we were, just a week out of the hospital, and he seemed to have changed his mind.

"Well, I guess he likes Dr. O'Holleran now," Sonja said.

Even if Colton had found it in his heart to forgive the good doctor, though, his little proclamation in the kitchen was weird. How many not-quite-four-year-olds analyze the family financial woes and demand payment for a creditor? Especially one he never particularly liked?

And the way he put it too: "Dad, Jesus used Dr. O'Holleran to help fix me." Weird.

Even weirder, though, was what happened next. With $23,000 in bills due and payable immediately, we didn't know what we were going to do. Sonja and I discussed asking our bank for a loan, but it turned out we didn't need to. First, my Grandma Ellen, who lives in Ulysses, Kansas, sent us a check to help with the hospital bills. Then, in a single week, more checks started arriving in the mail. Checks for $50, $100, $200, and all with cards and notes that said things like, "We heard about your troubles and we're praying for you," or "God put it on my heart to send you this. I hope it helps."

By the end of the week, our mailbox was full again—but with gifts, not bills. Church members, close friends, and even people who only knew us from a distance responded to our need without our even asking. The checks added up to thousands of dollars, and we were astonished when we found that, combined with what my grandmother sent, the total was what we needed to meet that first wave of bills, almost to the dollar.

~

Not long after Colton became a pint-size collection agent, he got in a little bit of trouble. Nothing huge, just an incident at a friend's house where he got into a tug-of-war over some toys. That evening, I called him to the kitchen table. I was sitting in a straight-back chair, and he climbed up in the chair beside me and knelt in it. Colton leaned on his elbows and regarded me with sky blue eyes that seemed a little bit sheepish.

If you have a preschooler, you know it can sometimes be hard to look past their cuteness and be serious about discipline. But I managed to put a serious look on my face. "Colton," I began, "do you know why you're in trouble?"

"Yeah. Because I didn't share," he said, casting his eyes down at the table.

"That's right. You can't do that, Colton. You've got to treat people better than that."

Colton raised his eyes and looked at me. "Yeah, I know, Dad. Jesus told me I had to be nice."

His words caught me a little by surprise. It was the way he said it: *Jesus told me . . .*

But I brushed it aside. *His Sunday school teachers must be doing a good job*, I thought.

"Well then, Jesus was right, wasn't he?" I said, and that was the end of it. I don't even think I gave Colton any consequences for not sharing. After all, with Jesus in the picture, I'd pretty much been outranked.

A couple of weeks later, I began preparing to preside over a funeral at church. The man who had passed away wasn't a member of our congregation, but people in town who don't attend services regularly often want a church funeral for a loved one. Sometimes the deceased is a friend or relative of a church member.

Colton must have heard Sonja and me discussing the upcoming service because he walked into the front room one morning and tugged on my shirttail. "Daddy, what's a funeral?"

I had done several funerals at church since Colton was born, but he was at that age where he was starting to become more interested in how and why things work.

"Well, buddy, a funeral happens when someone dies. A man here in town died, and his family is coming to the church to say good-bye to him."

Instantly, Colton's demeanor changed. His face fell into serious lines, and he stared fiercely into my eyes. "Did the man have Jesus in his heart?"

My son was asking me whether the man who had died was a Christian who had accepted Christ as his Savior. But his intensity caught me off guard. "I'm not sure, Colton," I said. "I didn't know him very well."

Colton's face bunched up in a terrible twist of worry. "He *had* to have Jesus in his heart! He *had* to know Jesus or he can't get into heaven!"

Again, his intensity surprised me, especially since he didn't even know this man. I tried to comfort him as best I could. "I've talked to some of the family members, and they told me he did," I said.

Colton didn't seem entirely convinced, but his face relaxed a bit. "Well . . . okay," he said and walked away.

For the second time in a couple of weeks, I thought, *Man, those Sunday school teachers sure are doing a good job!*

That weekend, Sonja dressed Cassie and Colton in their Sunday best, and we headed the half block down to the church to get ready for the funeral. As we pulled up in the SUV, I saw the Liewer Funeral Home hearse parked outside. Inside, we found the burnished oak casket standing off to one side of the foyer.

Two sets of open doorways led from the foyer into the sanctuary where the family was gathering for the "flower service." Before moving to Imperial, I'd never heard of a flower service, but now I think it's a really nice idea. The family gathers before the funeral service, and the funeral director points out each plant, wreath, and flower arrangement, explains who sent it, and reads aloud any message of sympathy attached. ("These beautiful purple azaleas come to you in loving memory from the Smith family.")

The pastor is supposed to be in the flower service. I peeked into the sanctuary and caught the funeral director's eye. He nodded, indicating they were ready to begin. I turned to gather Colton and Cassie, when Colton pointed to the casket. "What's that, Daddy?"

I tried to keep it simple. "That's the casket. The man who died is inside it."

Suddenly, Colton's face gathered into that same knot of intense concern. He slammed his fists on his thighs, then pointed one finger at the casket and said in a near shout, "Did that man have Jesus?!"

Sonja's eyes popped wide, and we both glanced at the sanctuary doorway, terrified the family inside could hear our son.

"He *had* to! He *had* to!" Colton went on. "He can't get into heaven if he didn't have Jesus in his heart!"

Sonja grabbed Colton by the shoulders and tried to shush him. But he was not shushable. Now nearly in tears, Colton twisted in her arms and yelled at me, "He *had* to know Jesus, Dad!"

Sonja steered him away from the sanctuary, hustling him toward the front doors of the church, with Cassie following. Through the glass doors, I could see Sonja bent down talking to Cassie and Colton outside. Then Cassie took her still-struggling brother by the hand and started walking the half block toward home.

I didn't know what to think. Where was this sudden concern over whether a stranger was saved, whether he "had Jesus in his heart," as Colton put it, coming from?

I did know this much: Colton was at that age where if something popped into his head, he'd just blurt it out. Like the time I took him to a restaurant in Madrid, Nebraska, and a guy with really long, straight hair walked in, and Colton asked loudly whether that was a boy or a girl. So we kept Colton away from funerals for a while if we didn't know for sure the deceased was a Christian. We just didn't know what he would say or do.

TWELVE

EYEWITNESS TO HEAVEN

It wasn't until four months after Colton's surgery, during our Fourth of July trip to meet our new nephew, that Sonja and I finally got a clue that something extraordinary had happened to our son. Sure, there had been a string of quirky things Colton had said and done since the hospital. Colton's insisting we pay Dr. O'Holleran because Jesus used the doctor to help "fix" him. His statement that Jesus "told" him he had to be good. And his strenuous, almost vehement funeral performance. But rushing by as brief scenes in the busyness of family life, those things just seemed . . . well, kind of cute. Except for the funeral thing, which was just plain weird.

But not *supernatural* weird. It wasn't until we were driving through North Platte on the way to South Dakota that the lights came on. You'll remember I was teasing Colton a little as we drove through town.

"Hey, Colton, if we turn here, we can go back to the hospital," I said. "Do you wanna go back to the hospital?"

It was that conversation in which Colton said that he "went up out of" his body, that he had spoken with angels, and had sat in Jesus' lap. And the way we knew he wasn't making it up was that he was able to tell us what we were doing in another part of the hospital: "You were in a little room by yourself praying, and Mommy was in a different room and she was praying and talking on the phone."

Not even Sonja had seen me in that little room, having my meltdown with God.

Suddenly, there in the Expedition on our holiday trip, the incidents of the past few months clicked into place like the last few quick twists in a Rubik's Cube solution: Sonja and I realized that this was not the first time Colton had let us know something amazing had happened to him; it was only the most clear-cut.

By the time we got to Sioux Falls, we were so busy getting to know our cute baby nephew, catching up on family news, and visiting the waterfall that we didn't have a lot of time to discuss Colton's strange revelations. But during the quiet moments before sleep, a flood of images tumbled through my mind—especially those horrible moments I'd spent in that tiny room at the hospital, raging against God. I thought I had been alone, pouring out my anger and grief in private. Staying strong for Sonja. But my son said he had seen me . . .

Our mini-vacation passed without any new disasters, and we returned to Imperial in time for me to preach on Sunday. The following week, Sonja and her friend Sherri Schoenholz headed to Colorado Springs for the Pike's Peak

Worship Festival, a conference on church music ministry. That left just me and the kids at home.

Like any prudent tornado-belt family, we have a basement below our one-story home. Ours is semifinished, with a small office and a bathroom that lead off a large, multipurpose, rumpus room area. Colton and I were down there one evening, as I worked on a sermon against the comforting background of my preschooler's action-figure war.

Colton was three years and ten months old at the time of his surgery, but in May we had celebrated his birthday, so he was now officially four. A big boy. The little party we had thrown was all the more special since we'd nearly lost him.

I don't remember exactly what day of the week it was when Colton and I were hanging out in the basement. But I do remember that it was evening and that Cassie wasn't there, so she must've been spending the night with a friend. As Colton played nearby, my attention drifted to our Arby's conversation about Jesus and the angels. I wanted to probe deeper, get him talking again. At that age, little boys don't exactly come up and offer you long, detailed histories. But they will answer direct questions, usually with direct answers. If Colton really had a supernatural encounter, I certainly didn't want to ask him leading questions. We had taught Colton about our faith all his life. But if he had really seen Jesus and the angels, I wanted to become the student, not the teacher!

Sitting at my makeshift desk, I looked over at my son as he brought Spider-Man pouncing down on some nasty-looking creature from Star Wars. "Hey, Colton," I said. "Remember when we were in the car and you talked about sitting on Jesus' lap?"

Still on his knees, he looked up at me. "Yeah."

"Well, did anything else happen?"

He nodded, eyes bright. "Did you know that Jesus has a cousin? Jesus told me his cousin baptized him."

"Yes, you're right," I said. "The Bible says Jesus' cousin's name is John."

Mentally, I scolded myself: *Don't offer information. Just let him talk . . .*

"I don't remember his name," Colton said happily, "but he was really nice."

John the Baptist is "nice"?!

Just as I was processing the implications of my son's statement—that he had *met* John the Baptist—Colton spied a plastic horse among his toys and held it up for me to look at. "Hey, Dad, did you know Jesus has a horse?"

"A horse?"

"Yeah, a rainbow horse. I got to pet him. There's lots of colors."

Lots of colors? What was he talking about?

"Where are there lots of colors, Colton?"

"In heaven, Dad. That's where all the rainbow colors are."

That set my head spinning. Suddenly I realized that up until that point, I'd been toying with the idea that maybe Colton had had some sort of divine visitation. Maybe Jesus and the angels had appeared to him in the hospital. I'd heard of similar phenomena many times when people were as near death as Colton had been. Now it was dawning on me that not only was my son saying he had left his body; *he was saying he had left the hospital!*

"You were in heaven?" I managed to ask.

"Well, yeah, Dad," he said, as if that fact should have been perfectly obvious.

I had to take a break. I stood and bounded up the stairs, picked up the phone, and dialed Sonja's cell. She picked up and I could hear music and singing in the background. "Do you know what your son just said to me?!"

"What?" she shouted over the noise.

"He told me he met John the Baptist!"

"What?"

I summarized the rest for her and could hear the amazement in her voice on the other end of the line.

She tried to press me for details, but the worship conference hall was too loud. Finally we had to give up. "Call me tonight after dinner, okay?" Sonja said. "I want to know everything!"

I hung up and leaned against the kitchen counter, processing. Slowly, I began to wrap my mind around the possibility that this was real. Had our son died and come back? The medical staff never gave any indication of that. But clearly, *something* had happened to Colton. He had authenticated that by telling us things he couldn't have known. It dawned on me that maybe we'd been given a gift and that our job now was to unwrap it, slowly, carefully, and see what was inside.

Back downstairs, Colton was still on his knees, bombing aliens. I sat down beside him.

"Hey, Colton, can I ask you something else about Jesus?"

He nodded but didn't look up from his devastating attack on a little pile of X-Men.

"What did Jesus look like?" I said.

Abruptly, Colton put down his toys and looked up at me. "Jesus has markers."

"What?"

"Markers, Daddy . . . Jesus has markers. And he has brown hair and he has hair on his face," he said, running his tiny palm around on his chin. I guessed that he didn't yet know the word *beard*. "And his eyes . . . oh, Dad, his eyes are *so* pretty!"

As he said this, Colton's face grew dreamy and far away, as if enjoying a particularly sweet memory.

"What about his clothes?"

Colton snapped back into the room and smiled at me. "He had purple on." As he said this, Colton put his hand on his left shoulder, moved it across his body down to his right hip then repeated the motion. "His clothes were white, but it was purple from here to here."

Another word he didn't know: *sash*.

"Jesus was the only one in heaven who had purple on, Dad. Did you know that?"

In Scripture, purple is the color of kings. A verse from the gospel of Mark flashed through my mind: "His clothes became dazzling white, whiter than anyone in the world could bleach them."[1]

"And he had this gold thing on his head . . ." Colton chirped on enthusiastically. He put both hands on top of his head in the shape of a circle.

"Like a crown?"

"Yeah, a crown, and it had this . . . this diamond thing in the middle of it and it was kind of pink. And he has markers, Dad."

My mind reeled. Here I'd thought I was leading my child gently down this conversational path but instead, he'd grabbed the reins and galloped away. Images from Scripture tumbled through my mind. The Christophany, or manifestation of Christ, in the book of Daniel, the appearance of the King of kings in Revelation. I was amazed that my son was describing Jesus in pretty much human terms—then amazed that I was amazed, since our whole faith revolves around the idea that man is made in God's image and Jesus both came to earth and returned to heaven as a man.

I knew by heart all the Bible stories we'd read him over the years, many from the Arch series, Bible storybooks I'd had as a child. And I knew our church's Sunday school lessons and how simplified they are in the preschool years: Jesus loves you. Be kind to others. God is good. If you could get a preschooler to take away just one three- or four-word concept on Sunday mornings, that was a huge accomplishment.

Now here was my kid, in his matter-of-fact, preschooler voice, telling me things that were not only astonishing on their face, but that also matched Scripture in every detail, right down to the rainbow colors described in the book of Revelation,[2] which is hardly preschool material. And as he babbled, Colton asked me, his pastor-dad, every so often, "Did you know that?"

And I'm thinking, *Yeah, but how do you know it?*

I sat in silence for a few moments as Colton resumed his bombing campaign. As would become a pattern for the next couple of years, I sat there and tried to figure out what to ask him next. I thought through what he had said so far . . . John the Baptist, Jesus and his clothes, rainbows, horses. I got all that. But what about the markers? What did Colton mean when he said Jesus has markers?

What are markers to a little kid?

Suddenly, I had it. "Colton, you said Jesus had markers. You mean like markers that you color with?"

Colton nodded. "Yeah, like colors. He had colors on him."

"Like when you color a page?"

"Yeah."

"Well, what color are Jesus' markers?"

"Red, Daddy. Jesus has red markers on him."

At that moment, my throat nearly closed with tears as I suddenly understood what Colton was trying to say. Quietly, carefully, I said, "Colton, where are Jesus' markers?"

Without hesitation, he stood to his feet. He held out his right hand, palm up and pointed to the center of it with his left. Then he held out his left palm and pointed with his right hand. Finally, Colton bent over and pointed to the tops of both his feet.

"That's where Jesus' markers are, Daddy," he said.

I drew in a sharp breath. *He* saw *this. He had to have.*

We know where the nails were driven when Jesus was crucified, but you don't spend a lot of time going over those gruesome facts with toddlers and preschoolers. In fact, I didn't know if my son had ever seen a crucifix. Catholic kids grow up with that image, but Protestant kids, especially young ones, just grow up with a general concept: "Jesus died on the cross."

I was also struck by how quickly Colton answered my questions. He spoke with the simple conviction of an eye-witness, not the carefulness of someone remembering the "right" answers learned in Sunday school or from a book.

"Colton, I'm going up to get some water," I said, really only wanting to exit the conversation. Whether or not he was done, I was done. I had enough information to chew on.

"Okay, Daddy," Colton said and bent to his toys.

Upstairs, in the kitchen, I leaned against the counter and sipped from a water bottle. *How could my little boy know this stuff?*

I knew he wasn't making it up. I was pretty sure neither Sonja nor I had ever talked to Colton about what Jesus wore at all, much less what he might be wearing in heaven. Could he have picked up such a detail from the Bible stories we read to the kids? More of Colton's knowledge about our faith came from that than from a month of Sundays. But again, the stories in the Bible storybooks we read to him were very narrative-oriented, and just a couple of hundred words each. Not at all heavy on details, like Jesus wearing white (yet Scripture says he did). And *no* details on what heaven might be like.

I took another sip of water and racked my brain about the cousin thing and the "markers." He didn't get that stuff from us. But even on the details I didn't understand at first, like the "markers," Colton was insistent. And there was another thing about the markers that nagged at me. When I asked

Colton what Jesus looked like, that was the first detail he popped out with. Not the purple sash, the crown, or even Jesus' eyes, with which Colton was clearly enchanted. He'd said, right off the bat, "Jesus has markers."

I'd once heard a spiritual "riddle" that went like this: "What's the only thing in heaven that's the same as it was on earth?"

The answer: the wounds in Jesus' hands and feet.

Maybe it was true.

THIRTEEN

LIGHTS AND WINGS

Sonja drove in from Colorado Springs on Saturday evening, and as we huddled in the living room over glasses of Pepsi, I filled her in on the rest of what Colton had said.

"What have we been missing?" I wondered aloud.

"I don't know," she said. "It's like he just pops out with new information all of a sudden."

"I want to know more, but I don't know what to ask him."

We were both teachers, Sonja in the formal sense and I in the pastoral sense. We agreed that the best way to proceed was to just keep asking open-ended questions as the situation presented itself, and not fill in any blanks for Colton as I had, inadvertently, when I suggested the word *crown* when Colton was describing the "gold thing" on Jesus' head. In the coming years, we would stick to that course so carefully that Colton didn't know the word *sash* until he was ten years old.

A couple of days after the conversation about the markers, I was sitting at the kitchen table, preparing for a sermon, and

Colton was playing nearby. I looked up from my books and over at my son, who was armed with plastic swords and in the process of tying the corners of a towel around his neck. Every superhero needs a cape.

I knew I wanted to ask him about heaven again and had been turning over possible questions in my mind. I had never had a conversation like this with Colton before, so I was a little nervous about how to begin. In fact, I had never had a conversation like this with *anyone* before.

Trying to catch him before he actually did battle, I got Colton's attention and motioned him to come sit with me. He trotted over and climbed into the chair at the end of the kitchen table. "Yes?"

"Remember when you were telling me what Jesus looks like? And about the horse?"

He nodded, eyes wide and earnest.

"You were in heaven?"

He nodded again.

I realized I was starting to accept that, yes, maybe Colton really had been to heaven. I felt like our family had received a gift and, having just peeled back the top layer of tissue paper, knew its general shape. Now I wanted to know what all was in the box.

"Well, what did you do in heaven?" I ventured.

"Homework."

Homework? That wasn't what I was expecting. Choir practice, maybe, but homework? "What do you mean?"

Colton smiled. "Jesus was my teacher."

"Like school?"

Colton nodded. "Jesus gave me work to do, and that was my favorite part of heaven. There were lots of kids, Dad."

This statement marked the beginning of a period that I wished we had written down. During this conversation and for the next year or so, Colton could name a lot of the kids he said were in heaven with him. He doesn't remember their names now, though, and neither do Sonja nor I.

This was also the first time Colton had mentioned other people in heaven. I mean, other than Bible figures like John the Baptist, but I have to admit that I sort of thought of him as . . . well, a "character" more than a regular person like you and me. It sounds kind of dumb since Christians talk all the time about going to heaven when we die. Why wouldn't I expect that Colton would've seen ordinary people?

But all I could think to ask was: "So what did the kids look like? What do people look like in heaven?"

"Everybody's got wings," Colton said.

Wings, huh?

"Did you have wings?" I asked.

"Yeah, but mine weren't very big." He looked a little glum when he said this.

"Okay . . . did you walk places or did you fly?"

"We flew. Well, all except for Jesus. He was the only one in heaven who didn't have wings. Jesus just went up and down like an elevator."

The book of Acts flashed into my head, the scene of Jesus' ascension, when Jesus told the disciples that they would be his witnesses, that they would tell people all over the world about him. After he said this, the Scripture says, Jesus "was taken up before their very eyes, and a cloud hid him from their sight. They were looking intently up into the sky as he was going, when suddenly two men dressed in white stood beside them. 'Men of Galilee,' they said, 'why do you stand here looking into the sky? This same Jesus, who has been taken from you into heaven, will come back in the same way you have seen him go into heaven.'"[1]

Jesus went up. And will come down. Without wings. To a kid, that could look like an elevator.

Colton broke into my thoughts. "Everyone kind of looks like angels in heaven, Dad."

"What do you mean?"

"All the people have a light above their head."

I racked my brain for what I knew about angels and light. In the Bible, when angels show up, they're sometimes dazzlingly bright, blinding almost. When Mary Magdalene and the other women showed up outside Jesus' tomb on the third day after he was buried, the gospels say that an angel met them, sitting on the tombstone that had somehow been rolled away: "His appearance was like lightning, and his clothes were white as snow."[2]

I remembered that the book of Acts talks about the disciple Stephen. As he was being accused of heresy before a Jewish court, they saw that "his face became as bright as an angel's."[3] Not long after, Stephen was stoned to death.

The apostle John in the book of Revelation, wrote that he saw a "mighty angel coming down from heaven, surrounded by a cloud, with a rainbow over his head," and that the angel's face "shone like the sun."[4]

I couldn't remember angels having *lights* over their heads specifically—or halos, as some would call them—but I also knew that Colton's experience of angels in storybooks and Scripture did not include lights over angels' heads. And he didn't even know the word *halo*. I don't know that he'd ever even seen one, since our bedtime Bible stories and the Sunday school lessons at church are closely aligned with Scripture.

Still, what he said intrigued me for another reason: A friend of ours, the wife of a pastor at a church in Colorado, had once told me about something her daughter, Hannah, said when she was three years old. After the morning service was over one Sunday, Hannah tugged on her mom's skirt and asked, "Mommy, why do some people in church have lights over their heads and some don't?"

At the time, I remember thinking two things: First, I would've knelt down and asked Hannah, "Did *I* have a light over my head? Please say yes!"

I also wondered what Hannah had seen, and whether she had seen it because, like my son, she had a childlike faith.

When the disciples asked Jesus who is the greatest in the kingdom of heaven, Jesus called a little boy from the crowd and had him stand among them as an example. "I tell you the truth," Jesus said, "unless you change and become like little children, you will never enter the kingdom of heaven. Therefore, whoever humbles himself like this child is the greatest in the kingdom of heaven."[5]

Whoever humbles himself like this child . . .

What is childlike humility? It's not the lack of intelligence, but the lack of guile. The lack of an agenda. It's that precious,

Colton's three-year-old preschool
photo, October 2002

The Imperial Republican/Ian Schultz

Doc's Dodgers, Todd and Sonja's coed softball team

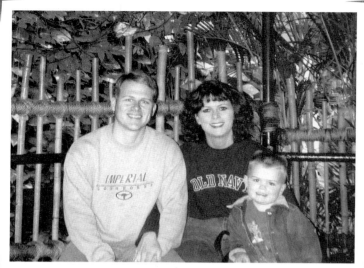

Todd, Sonja, and Colton at the Denver Butterfly Pavilion,
March 1, 2003

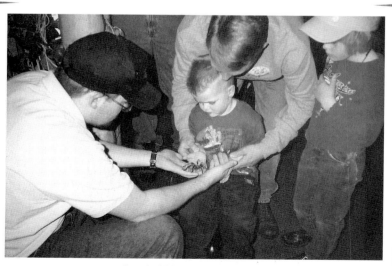

Colton holding Rosie the tarantula
with older sister Cassie watching

Photo from the *Imperial Republican* newspaper, Colton
and Todd one week after Colton's hospital release

Colton's 4th birthday party, a real
celebration! May 19, 2003

Colton, Todd, Sonja, and Cassie at Sioux Falls,
South Dakota, July 2003

Colton's first day of
second year preschool,
September 2003

Todd and Colton,
November 2003

Colton at age seven and Colby at eighteen months
playing swords, Spring 2006

Colton, aka The Flash, October 2007

Lawrence Barber, "Pop," at age 29 with Grandma Ellen,
Uncle Bill, and Todd's mom, Kay, 1943

Lawrence Barber, "Pop," at age 61

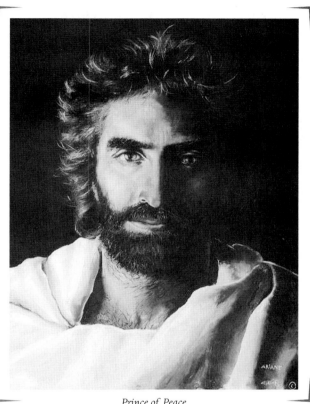

Prince of Peace
by Akiane Kramarik

Cassie, Todd, Colby, Sonja, and Colton at Todd's
cowboy-themed 40th birthday party, August 2008

fleeting time before we have accumulated enough pride or
position to care what other people might think. The same
un-self-conscious honesty that enables a three-year-old to
splash joyfully in a rain puddle, or tumble laughing in the
grass with a puppy, or point out loudly that you have a booger
hanging out of your nose, is what is required to enter heaven.
It is the opposite of ignorance—it is intellectual honesty: to
be willing to accept reality and to call things what they are
even when it is hard.

All this flashed through my mind in an instant, but I
remained noncommittal.

"A light, huh?" was all I said.

"Yeah, and they have yellow from here to here," he said,
making the sash motion again, left shoulder to right hip. "And
white from here to here." He placed his hands on his shoulders, then bent forward and touched the tops of his feet.

I thought of the "man" who appeared to the prophet
Daniel: "On the twenty-fourth day of the first month, as I was
standing on the bank of the great river, the Tigris, I looked up
and there before me was a man dressed in linen, with a belt of
the finest gold around his waist. His body was like chrysolite,
his face like lightning, his eyes like flaming torches, his arms
and legs like the gleam of burnished bronze."[6]

Colton then made the sash motion again and said that
people in heaven wore different colors there than the
angels did.

By now my New Information Meter was nearly pegged,
but there was one more thing I had to know. If Colton really
had been to heaven and really had seen all these things—Jesus,

horses, angels, other children—and was up there (was it *up*?) long enough to *do homework*, how long had he "left" his body, as he claimed?

I looked at him, kneeling in the kitchen chair with his towel-cape still tied around his neck. "Colton, you said you were in heaven and you did all these things . . . a *lot* of things. How long were you gone?"

My little boy looked me right in the eye and didn't hesitate. "Three minutes," he said. Then he hopped down from the chair and skipped off to play.

FOURTEEN

ON HEAVEN TIME

Three minutes?

As Colton began to set up for an epic plastic-sword fight with an unseen villain, I marveled at his answer.

He had already authenticated his experience by telling me things he could not otherwise have known. But now I had to square his answer, "three minutes," with all the rest. I stared down at my Bible, lying open on the kitchen table, and turned over the possibilities in my mind.

Three minutes. It wasn't possible that Colton could have seen and done everything he'd described so far in just three minutes. Of course, he wasn't old enough to tell time yet, so maybe his sense of three *actual* minutes wasn't the same as an adult's. Like most parents, I was pretty sure Sonja and I weren't helping that issue, promising to be off the phone, for example, or finished talking in the yard with a neighbor, or done in the garage in "five more minutes," then wrapping it up *twenty* minutes later.

It was also possible that time in heaven doesn't track with time on earth. The Bible says that with the Lord, "a day is like a thousand years, and a thousand years are like a day."[1] Some interpret that as a literal exchange, as in, two days equals two thousand years. I've always taken it to mean that God operates outside of our understanding of time. Time on earth is keyed to a celestial clock, governed by the solar system. But the Bible says there is no sun in heaven because God is the light there. Maybe there is no time in heaven. At least not as we understand it.

On the other hand, Colton's "three minutes" answer was as straight up and matter-of-fact as if he'd told me he'd had Lucky Charms for breakfast. As far as our clock goes, he could've been right. For him to leave his body and return to it, he couldn't have been gone long. Especially since we'd never received any kind of report saying Colton had ever been clinically dead. In fact, the postoperative report was clear that even though our son's prognosis had been grim, the surgery had gone just fine:

OPERATIVE REPORT

OPERATIVE DATE: 3/5/2003

PREOPERATIVE DIAGNOSIS: Acute appendicitis

POSTOPERATIVE DIAGNOSIS: Perforated appendicitis and abscess

OPERATION: Appendectomy and drainage of abscess

SURGEON: Timothy O'Holleran, M.D.

DESCRIPTION OF THE OPERATION: The patient was placed in a supine position on the Operating Table. Under general anesthesia the abdomen was prepped and draped in a sterile fashion. A transverse incision was made in the right lower quadrant and carried down through all layers in the peritoneal cavity. . . . The patient had a perforated appendix with an abscess. The appendix was delivered up in the operative field.

A thought hit me like a brick: *Colton didn't die.*

How could he have gone to heaven if he didn't die?

A couple of days passed as I chewed on that. It had only been a week or so since Colton first told us about the angels, so I didn't want to keep pushing the heaven issue. But finally, I couldn't stand it anymore and hunted the house for Colton until I found him, down on his knees in the bedroom we'd converted to a playroom, building a tower of LEGOs. I leaned in the door frame and got his attention.

"Hey, Colton, I don't understand," I began.

He looked up at me, and I noticed for the first time that all the roundness had returned to his face, his cheeks filled out and rosy again after his illness had drained them thin and sallow. "What?"

"You said you went to heaven. People have to die to go to heaven."

Colton's gaze didn't waver. "Well, okay then, I died. But just for a little bit."

My heart skipped a beat. If you haven't heard your pre-schooler tell you he was dead, I don't recommend it. But Colton hadn't died. I knew what the medical record said. Colton had never ceased breathing. His heart had never stopped.

I stood in the doorway and mulled over this new tidbit as

Colton returned his attention to his toys. Then I remembered that the Bible talks in several places about people who had seen heaven *without* dying. The apostle Paul wrote to the church at Corinth about a Christian he knew personally who was taken to heaven, "Whether it was in the body or out of the body I do not know—God knows. And I know that this man . . . was caught up to paradise. He heard inexpressible things, things that man is not permitted to tell."[2]

Then, of course, there was John the apostle, who described heaven in great detail in the book of Revelation. John had been exiled to the island of Patmos, where an angel visited him and commanded him to write down a series of prophecies to various churches. John wrote:

> After this I looked, and there before me was a door standing open in heaven. And the voice I had first heard speaking to me like a trumpet said, "Come up here, and I will show you what must take place after this." At once I was in the Spirit, and there before me was a throne in heaven with someone sitting on it. And the one who sat there had the appearance of jasper and carnelian. A rainbow, resembling an emerald, encircled the throne.[3]

Rainbows . . . now where had I heard that recently?

As I stood there and thought through a scriptural basis for experiencing heaven without dying, I realized that Colton, in telling me he had died "for a little bit," had only been trying to match up his pastor-dad's assertion with what he knew to be the facts of his own experience. Kind of like walking outside and finding that the street is wet, and concluding, well, okay, it must have rained.

See, I had this tidy little box that said, "People have to die to go to heaven," and Colton, trusting me, concluded, "Well, I must have died then, because I was there."

Suddenly, he piped up again. "Daddy, remember when I yelled for you in the hospital when I waked up?"

How could I forget? It was the most beautiful sound I'd ever heard. "Of course I do," I said.

"Well, the reason I was yelling was that Jesus came to get me. He said I had to go back because he was answering your prayer. That's how come I was yelling for you."

Suddenly, my knees felt weak underneath me. I flashed back to my prayers alone, raging at God, and my prayers in the waiting room, quiet and desperate. I remembered how scared I was, agonizing over whether Colton would hang on through the surgery, whether he'd live long enough for me to see his precious face again. Those were the longest, darkest ninety minutes of my life.

And Jesus answered my prayer? Personally? After I had yelled at God, chastising him, questioning his wisdom and his faithfulness?

Why would God even answer a prayer like that? And how did I deserve his mercy?

FIFTEEN

CONFESSION

The first weeks of July burned into the plains, nurturing the cornfields with all the heat of a giant greenhouse. Wedgewood blue skies arced over Imperial almost every day, the air buzzing with mosquitoes in the sunshine and singing with crickets by starlight. Around the middle of July, I drove over to Greeley, Colorado, for the church district conference. The gathering of about 150 pastors, pastors' wives, and delegates from Nebraska and Colorado was meeting at the church pastored by Steve Wilson—the same church I'd visited back in March while Sonja stayed back at the Harrises' home, nursing Colton when we all thought he had a stomach flu.

Roman Catholics practice confession as a sacrament, sharing their sins and shortcomings with a priest. Protestants practice confession, too, though a little less formally, often confiding in God without an intermediary. But Colton's recent revelation that my raging prayers had ascended directly to heaven—and had received an equally direct response—made me feel like I had some additional confessing to do.

I didn't feel good about having been so angry with God. When I was so upset, burning with righteous anger that he was about to take my child, guess who was holding my child? Guess who was loving my child, unseen? As a pastor, I felt accountable to other pastors for my own lack of faith. So at Greeley Wesleyan during the conference, I asked Phil Harris, our district superintendent, if I could have a few minutes to share.

He agreed, and when the time came, I stood up before my peers in the sanctuary that on Sunday mornings held around a thousand people in its pews. After delivering a brief update on Colton's health, I thanked these men and women for their prayers on behalf of our family. Then I began my confession.

"Most of you know that before everything happened with Colton, I had broken my leg and gone through the kidney stone operation, then the lumpectomy. I had had such a bad year that some people had started calling me Pastor Job."

The sanctuary echoed with gentle laughter.

"But none of that stuff hurt like watching what Colton was going through, and I got really mad at God," I continued. "I'm a guy. Guys *do* something. And all I felt like I could do was yell at God."

I described briefly my attitude in that little room in the hospital, blasting God, blaming him for Colton's condition, whining about how he had chosen to treat one of his pastors, as though I should somehow be exempt from troubles because I was doing "his" work.

"At that time, when I was so upset and so outraged, can you believe that God chose to answer that prayer?" I said.

"Can you believe that I could pray a prayer like that, and God would still answer it 'yes'?"

What had I learned? I was reminded yet again that I could be real with God, I told my fellow pastors. I learned that I didn't have to offer some kind of churchy, holy-sounding prayer in order to be heard in heaven. "You might as well tell God what you think," I said. "He already knows it anyway."

Most importantly of all, I learned that *I am heard*. We all are. I had been a Christian since childhood and a pastor for half my life, so I believed that before. But now I *knew* it. How? As the nurses wheeled my son away screaming, "Daddy, Daddy, don't let them take me!" . . . when I was angry at God because I couldn't go to my son, hold him, and comfort him, God's son was holding my son in his lap.

SIXTEEN

POP

On a sun-drenched day in August, four-year-old Colton hopped into the passenger seat of my red pickup, and the two of us headed off to Benkelman. I had to drive out there to bid a job and decided to take Colton with me. He wasn't particularly interested in the installation of industrial-sized garage doors. But he loved riding in my little Chevy diesel because, unlike the Expedition where he had a limited view from the backseat, his car seat rode high in the Chevy, and he could see everything.

Benkelman is a small farming town thirty-eight miles due south of Imperial. Incorporated in 1887, it's fraying a bit at the edges like a lot of communities in rural Nebraska, its population declining as technology eats up agricultural jobs and people move to bigger cities in search of work. I steered past the familiar fertilizer and potato plants that rise at the east end of Imperial, then turned south toward Enders Lake. We drove by the cedar-dotted municipal golf course on our left, and then, as we passed over a concrete dam, the lake sparkled

below on our right. Colton looked down at a speedboat tow-
ing a skier in its foamy wake. We crossed the dam, dipped
down in a valley, and motored up onto the stretch of two-lane
highway that points straight south. Now acres of farmland
fanned out around us, cornstalks six feet high bright green
against the sky, and the asphalt cutting through it like a blade.

Suddenly Colton spoke up. "Dad, you had a grandpa
named Pop, didn't you?"

"Yep, sure did," I said.

"Was he your mommy's daddy or your daddy's daddy?"

"Pop was my mom's dad. He passed away when I was not
much older than you."

Colton smiled. "He's really nice."

I almost drove off the road into the corn. It's a crazy
moment when your son uses the present tense to refer to
someone who died a quarter century before he was even
born. But I tried to stay cool. "So you saw Pop?" I said.

"Yeah, I got to stay with him in heaven. You were really
close to him, huh, Dad?"

"Yes, I was," was all I could manage. My head spun.
Colton had just introduced a whole new topic: people
you've lost, and meeting them in heaven. Crazily enough,
with all the talk of Jesus and angels and horses, I had never
even thought to ask him if he'd met anyone *I* might know.
But then, why would I? We hadn't lost any family or friends
since Colton was born, so who would there have been for
him to meet?

Now this. I probably drove another ten miles toward
Benkelman, thoughts charging through my mind. Soon, the

cornfields were broken by neat squares of bronzed stubble, wheat fields past the harvest.

I didn't want to make the same mistake I'd made when I'd put ideas in his head—that people had to die, for example, before being admitted to heaven. I didn't want him just feeding me back stuff to please me. I wanted to know the truth.

On the left, a quarter mile off the road, a white church steeple seemed to rise from the corn. St. Paul's Lutheran Church, built in 1918. I wondered what the people of this longstanding local fixture would think of the things our little boy had been telling us.

Finally, as we crossed into Dundy County, I was ready to start asking some open-ended questions. "Hey, Colton," I said.

He turned from the window where he'd been watching a pheasant pacing us amid the corn rows. "What?"

"Colton, what did Pop look like?"

He broke into a big grin. "Oh, Dad, Pop has really big wings!"

Again with the present tense. It was weird.

Colton went on. "My wings were really little, but Pop's were big!"

"What did his clothes look like?"

"He had white on, but blue here," he said, making the sash motion again.

I edged the truck over to avoid a ladder someone had dropped in the road then steered back to the center of the lane. "And you got to stay with Pop?"

Colton nodded, and his eyes seemed to light up.

"When I was a little boy," I said, "I had a lot of fun with Pop."

I didn't tell Colton why I spent so much time with Pop and my Grandma Ellen on their farm in Ulysses, Kansas. The sad truth was that my dad, a chemist who worked for Kerr-McGee Petroleum, suffered from bipolar disorder. Sometimes, when his episodes got bad enough, my mom, Kay, an elementary school teacher, had to put Dad in the hospital. She sent me to Pop's to shield me from that. I didn't know I was being "shipped away"—I just knew I loved roaming the farm, chasing chickens, and hunting rabbits.

"I spent a lot of time with Pop at their place out in the country," I said to Colton. "I rode on the combine and the tractor with him. He had a dog, and we'd take him out and hunt rabbits."

Colton nodded again: "Yeah, I know! Pop told me."

Well, I didn't know what to say to that, so I said, "The dog's name was Charlie Brown, and he had one blue eye and one brown one."

"Cool!" Colton said. "Can we get a dog like that?"

I chuckled. "We'll see."

My grandfather, Lawrence Barber, was a farmer and one of those people who knew everyone and whom everyone considered a friend. He started most of his days before dawn, beating it from his farmhouse in Ulysses, Kansas, down to the local doughnut shop to swap stories. He was a big guy; he played fullback in the days before the pass. His wife, my Grandma Ellen (the same grandma who sent money to help with Colton's hospital bills), used to say it would take four or five tacklers to bring Lawrence Barber down.

Pop was a guy who went to church only once in a while. He was kind of private about spiritual things, the way a lot of men tend to be. I was about six years old when he died after driving off the road late one night. Pop's Crown Victoria hit a power pole, cracking it in half. The top half of the pole keeled over and smashed into the Crown Victoria's roof, but the car's momentum carried Pop another half mile into a field. The accident knocked out the power at a feed yard a little way back in the direction Pop had come from, prompting a worker there to investigate. Pop was apparently alive and breathing right after the accident, because rescue workers found him stretched across the passenger seat, reaching for the door handle to try to escape from the car. But when he arrived by ambulance at the hospital, doctors pronounced him dead. He was only sixty-one years old.

I remember seeing my mother in anguish at the funeral, but her grief didn't end there. As I got older, I'd sometimes catch her in prayer, with tears gently sliding down her cheeks. When I asked her what was wrong, she would share with me, "I'm worried about whether Pop went to heaven."

We didn't find out until much later, in 2006, from my Aunt Connie, about a special service Pop had attended only two days before his death—a service that might hold answers to my grandfather's eternal destiny.

The date was July 13, 1975, and the place was Johnson, Kansas. Mom and Aunt Connie had an uncle named Hubert Caldwell. I liked Uncle Hubert. Not only was Hubert a simple country preacher, but he loved to talk and was the type who was easy to talk to. (I also enjoyed Hubert because he was short, shorter than me. Looking down to visit with anyone happens so rarely for me that even the opportunity feels like a privilege.)

Uncle Hubert had invited Pop, Connie, and many others to revival services he was leading in his little country church. From behind his pulpit at the Church of God of Apostolic Faith, Hubert closed his message by asking if anyone wanted to give his life to Christ. Uncle Hubert saw Pop raise his hand. But somehow, that story never made it back to my mom, and she worried about it off and on for the next twenty-eight years.

After we got home from Benkelman, I called my mom and told her what Colton had said. That was on a Friday. The next morning, she pulled into our driveway, having made the trip all the way from Ulysses to hear what her grandson had to say about her dad. It surprised us how quickly she arrived.

"Boy, she beelined it up here!" Sonja said.

Around the dinner table that evening, Sonja and I listened as Colton told his grandma about Jesus' rainbow horse and spending time with Pop. The thing that surprised Mom most was the way Colton told the story: Pop had recognized his great-grandson even though Colton was born decades after Pop died. That got Mom wondering whether those who have gone ahead of us know what's happening on earth. Or is it that in heaven, we'll know our loved ones—even those we didn't get to meet in life—by some next-life way of knowing we don't enjoy on earth?

Then Mom asked Colton an odd question. "Did Jesus say anything about your dad becoming a pastor?"

Just as I was wondering privately why in the world something like my vocation would even come up, Colton surprised me when he nodded enthusiastically. "Oh, yes! Jesus said he went to Daddy and told him he wanted Daddy to be a pastor and Daddy said yes, and Jesus was really happy."

I just about fell out of my chair. That was true, and I vividly remember the night it happened. I was thirteen years old and attending a summer youth camp at John Brown University in Siloam Springs, Arkansas. At one of the evening meetings, Rev. Orville Butcher delivered a message about how God calls people to ministry and uses them to do his work all over the world.

Pastor Butcher was a short, bald, lively preacher—energetic and engaging, not dull and dry the way kids sometimes expect an older pastor to be. He challenged the group of 150 teenagers that night: "There are some of you here tonight whom God could use as pastors and missionaries."

The memory of that moment of my life is one of those crystal-clear ones, distilled and distinct, like the moment you graduate from high school or your first child is born. I remember that the crowd of kids faded away and the reverend's voice receded into the background. I felt a pressure in my heart, almost a whisper: *That's you, Todd. That's what I want you to do.*

There was no doubt in my mind that I had just heard from God. I was determined to obey. I tuned back in to Pastor Butcher just in time to hear him say that if any of us had heard from God that night, if any of us had made a commitment to serve him in ministry, we should tell someone about it when we got home so that at least one other person would know. So when I got home from camp, I walked into the kitchen.

"Mom," I said, "when I grow up, I'm going to be a pastor."

Since that day decades before, Mom and I had revisited that conversation a couple of times. But we had never told Colton about it.

SEVENTEEN

TWO SISTERS

As the green days of summer gave way to a fiery fall, we talked with Colton about heaven every now and then. But one running conversation did emerge: when Colton saw Jesus in heaven, what did he look like? The reason for the frequency of this particular topic was that as a pastor, I wound up spending a lot of time at hospitals, in Christian bookstores, and at other churches—all places where there are lots of drawings and paintings of Christ. Often, Sonja and the kids were with me, so it became sort of a game. When we came across a picture of Jesus, we'd ask Colton, "What about this one? Is that what Jesus looks like?"

Invariably, Colton would peer for a moment at the picture and shake his tiny head. "No, the hair's not right," he would say. Or, "The clothes aren't right."

This would happen dozens of times over the next three years. Whether it was a poster in a Sunday school room, a rendering of Christ on a book cover, or a reprint of an old master's painting hanging on the wall of an old folks' home,

Colton's reaction was always the same: He was too young to articulate exactly what was wrong with every picture; he just knew they weren't right.

One evening in October, I was sitting at the kitchen table, working on a sermon. Sonja was around the corner in the living room, working on the business books, processing job tickets, and sorting through payables. Cassie played Barbie dolls at her feet. I heard Colton's footsteps padding up the hallway and caught a glimpse of him circling the couch, where he then planted himself directly in front of Sonja.

"Mommy, I have two sisters," Colton said.

I put down my pen. Sonja didn't. She kept on working.

Colton repeated himself. "Mommy, I have two sisters."

Sonja looked up from her paperwork and shook her head slightly. "No, you have your sister, Cassie, and . . . do you mean your cousin, Traci?"

"No." Colton clipped off the word adamantly. "I have two *sisters*. You had a baby die in your tummy, didn't you?"

At that moment, time stopped in the Burpo household, and Sonja's eyes grew wide. Just a few seconds before, Colton had been trying unsuccessfully to get his mom to listen to him. Now, even from the kitchen table, I could see that he had her undivided attention.

"Who told you I had a baby die in my tummy?" Sonja said, her tone serious.

"She did, Mommy. She said she died in your tummy."

Then Colton turned and started to walk away. He had said what he had to say and was ready to move on. But after the bomb he'd just dropped, Sonja was just getting started. Before our son could get around the couch, Sonja's voice rang out in an all-hands-on-deck red alert. *"Colton Todd Burpo, you get back here right now!"*

Colton spun around and caught my eye. His face said, *What did I just do?*

I knew what my wife had to be feeling. Losing that baby was the most painful event of her life. We had explained it to Cassie; she was older. But we hadn't told Colton, judging the topic a bit beyond a four-year-old's capacity to understand. From the table, I watched quietly as emotions rioted across Sonja's face.

A bit nervously, Colton slunk back around the couch and faced his mom again, this time much more warily. "It's okay, Mommy," he said. "She's okay. God adopted her."

Sonja slid off the couch and knelt down in front of Colton so that she could look him in the eyes. "Don't you mean Jesus adopted her?" she said.

"No, Mommy. His Dad did!"

Sonja turned and looked at me. In that moment, she later told me, she was trying to stay calm, but she was overwhelmed. *Our baby . . . was—is!—a girl*, she thought.

Sonja focused on Colton, and I could hear the effort it took to steady her voice. "So what did she look like?"

"She looked a lot like Cassie," Colton said. "She is just a little bit smaller, and she has dark hair."

Sonja's dark hair.

As I watched, a blend of pain and joy played across my wife's face. Cassie and Colton have my blond hair. She had even jokingly complained to me before, "I carry these kids

for *nine months*, and they both come out looking like you!"
Now there was a child who looked like her. A daughter. I saw
the first hint of moisture glint in my wife's eyes.

Now Colton went on without prompting. "In heaven, this
little girl ran up to me, and she wouldn't stop hugging me,"
he said in a tone that clearly indicated he didn't enjoy all this
hugging from a *girl*.

"Maybe she was just happy that someone from her family was there," Sonja offered. "Girls hug. When we're happy,
we hug."

Colton didn't seem convinced.

Sonja's eyes lit up and she asked, "What was her name?
What was the little girl's name?"

Colton seemed to forget about all the yucky girl hugs for a
moment. "She doesn't have a name. You guys didn't name her."

How did he know that?

"You're right, Colton," Sonja said. "We didn't even know
she was a she."

Then Colton said something that still rings in my ears:
"Yeah, she said she just can't wait for you and Daddy to get to
heaven."

From the kitchen table, I could see that Sonja was barely
holding it together. She gave Colton a kiss and told him he
could go play. And when he left the room, tears spilled over
her cheeks.

"Our baby is okay," she whispered. "Our baby is okay."

From that moment on, the wound from one of the most
painful episodes in our lives, losing a child we had wanted very
much, began to heal. For me, losing the baby was a terrible

blow. But Sonja had told me that to her, the miscarriage not only seared her heart with grief, but it also felt like a personal failure.

"You do all the right things, eat all the right things, and you pray for the baby's health, but still this tiny baby dies inside you," she had once told me. "I feel guilty. I know in my mind that it wasn't my fault, but there's still this guilt."

We had wanted to believe that our unborn child had gone to heaven. Even though the Bible is largely silent on this point, we had accepted it on faith. But now, we had an eyewitness: a daughter we had never met was waiting eagerly for us in eternity. From then on, Sonja and I began to joke about who would get to heaven first. There were several reasons she had always wanted to outlive me. For one thing, a pastor's wife has to put up with being used as a sermon illustration a lot. If I died first, she's always told me, she'd finally get to tell the congregation all *her* stories about *me*.

But now Sonja had a reason for wanting to reach heaven first. When she was pregnant with the child we lost, we had picked out a boy's name—Colton—but we never could agree on a name for a little girl. I liked Kelsey, she liked Caitlin, and neither of us would budge.

But now that we know our little girl doesn't have a name yet, we constantly tell each other, "I'm going to beat you to heaven and name her first!"

EIGHTEEN

THE THRONE ROOM OF GOD

One night near Christmas 2003, I followed Colton into his room at bedtime. According to our usual routine, he picked a Bible story for me to read to him, and that night it was *The Wise King and the Baby*. The story was based on the one in the book of 1 Kings in which two women live together, and each one has an infant son. During the night, one of the babies dies. Overcome with grief, the mother of the dead child tries to claim the other boy as her own. The real mother of the living boy tries to convince the grieving mother of the truth but can't persuade her to give up the surviving baby. Desperate to get her child back, the mother of the living boy suggests that King Solomon, widely known for his wisdom, could settle the matter and determine who the real mother was of the living infant. In the biblical story, King Solomon devises a way to find out what is in each woman's heart.

"Cut the child in half!" the king decrees. "Give half to one and half to the other."

The grieving mother agrees to the solution, but the real mother reveals her love, crying out, "No! Let her have the child!" And that's how the wise king figured out which mother was telling the truth, and it's where we get the common phrase, "a Solomonic solution."

I came to the end of the story, and Colton and I had our usual good-natured argument over reading it again (and again and again). This time, I won. As we knelt on the floor to pray, I laid the book aside on the carpet, and it fell open to an illustration that pictured King Solomon sitting on his throne. It dawned on me that the Bible talks about God's throne in several places. For example, the author of the book of Hebrews urges believers to "approach the throne of grace with confidence,"[1] and says that after Jesus had completed his work on earth, he "sat down at the right hand of the throne of God."[2] And there's that glorious chapter in the book of Revelation that describes God's throne:

> I saw the Holy City, the new Jerusalem, coming down out of heaven from God, prepared as a bride beautifully dressed for her husband. And I heard a loud voice from the throne saying, "Now the dwelling of God is with men, and he will live with them. They will be his people, and God himself will be with them and be their God. He will wipe every tear from their eyes. There will be no more death or mourning or crying or pain, for the old order of things has passed away."
>
> He who was seated on the throne said, "I am making everything new!" . . .

I did not see a temple in the city, because the Lord God Almighty and the Lamb are its temple. The city does not need the sun or the moon to shine on it, for the glory of God gives it light, and the Lamb is its lamp.³

"Hey, Colton," I said, kneeling next to him, "when you were in heaven, did you ever see God's throne?"

Colton looked at me quizzically. "What's a throne, Daddy?"

I picked up the Bible storybook and pointed to the picture of Solomon seated in his court. "A throne is like the king's chair. It's the chair that only the king can sit in."

"Oh, yeah! I saw that a bunch of times!" Colton said.

My heart sped up a little. Was I really going to get a glimpse into the throne room of heaven? "Well, what did God's throne look like?"

"It was big, Dad . . . *really, really* big, because God is the biggest one there is. And he really, really loves us, Dad. You can't *belieeeeve* how much he loves us!"

When he said this, a contrast struck me: Colton, a little guy, was talking about a being so big—but in the next breath, he was talking about love. For one thing, God's size clearly wasn't scary to Colton, but it was also interesting to me that as eager as Colton was to tell about what God *looked* like, he was just as eager to tell me what God *felt* like toward us.

"And do you know that Jesus sits right next to God?" Colton went on excitedly. "Jesus' chair is right next to his Dad's!"

That blew me away. There's no way a four-year-old knows

that. It was another one of those moments when I thought, *He had to have seen this.*

I was pretty sure he had never even heard of the book of Hebrews, but there was one way to find out.

"Colton, which side of God's throne was Jesus sitting on?" I asked.

Colton climbed up on the bed and faced me on his knees. "Well, pretend like you're in God's throne. Jesus sat right there," he said, pointing to my right side.

The Hebrews passage flashed into my mind: "Let us fix our eyes on Jesus, the author and perfecter of our faith, who for the joy set before him endured the cross, scorning its shame, and sat down at the right hand of the throne of God."[4]

Wow. Here was a rare case where I had tested Colton's memories against what the Bible says, and he passed without batting an eye. But now I had another question, one I didn't know the answer to, at least not an answer from the Bible.

"Well, who sits on the other side of God's throne?" I said.

"Oh, that's easy, Dad. That's where the angel Gabriel is. He's really nice."

Gabriel. That makes sense. I remembered the story of John the Baptist and the moment when Gabriel arrived to deliver the news of John the Baptist's coming birth.

But the angel said to him: "Do not be afraid, Zechariah; your prayer has been heard. Your wife Elizabeth will bear you a son, and you are to give him the name John. He will be a joy and delight to you, and many will rejoice because of his birth, for he will be great in the sight of the Lord. . . ."

Zechariah asked the angel, "How can I be sure of this? I am an old man and my wife is well along in years."

The angel answered, "I am Gabriel. I stand in the presence of God, and I have been sent to speak to you and to tell you this good news."[5]

"I stand in the presence of God," Gabriel told Zechariah. And now, more than two thousand years later, my little boy was telling me the same thing.

So I'd had my glimpse into God's throne room, but Colton's descriptions had me wondering: if God the Father was seated on his throne with Jesus on his right and Gabriel on his left, where was Colton?

Colton had already crawled underneath his blanket, his blond head nestled against a Spider-Man pillowcase. "Where did you sit, Colton?" I asked.

"They brought in a little chair for me," he said, smiling. "I sat by God the Holy Spirit. Did you know that God is three persons, Dad?"

"Yeah, I think I know that one," I said and smiled.

"I was sitting by God the Holy Spirit because I was praying for you. You needed the Holy Spirit, so I prayed for you."

This took my breath away. Colton saying that he was praying for me in heaven reminded me of the letter to the Hebrews, where the writer says: "Therefore, since we are surrounded by such a great cloud of witnesses . . . let us run with perseverance the race marked out for us."[6]

"What does God look like?" I said. "God the Holy Spirit?"

Colton furrowed his brow. "Hmm, that's kind of a hard one . . . he's kind of blue."

Just as I was trying to picture that, Colton shifted course again. "You know, that's where I met Pop."

"You met Pop sitting by the Holy Spirit?"

Colton nodded vigorously, smiling at what seemed a pleasant memory. "Yep. Pop came up to me and said, 'Is Todd your dad?' And I said yes. And Pop said, 'He's my grandson.'"

How many times, when I presided over a funeral, had mourners delivered the usual well-meaning platitudes: "Well, she's in a better place," or "We know he's looking down on us, smiling," or "You'll see him again." Of course, I believed those things in theory, but to be honest, I couldn't picture them. Now, with what Colton had said about Pop and about his sister, I began to think about heaven in a different way. Not just a place with jeweled gates, shining rivers, and streets of gold, but a realm of joy and fellowship, both for those who are with us in eternity and those still on earth, whose arrival we eagerly anticipated. A place where I would one day walk and talk with my grandfather who had meant so much to me, and with the daughter I had never met.

With all my heart, I wanted to believe. At that moment, the details of our conversations began to pile up in my mind like a stack of Polaroids—pictures of heaven that seemed uncannily accurate from the descriptions we all have available to us in the Bible—all of us who can *read*, that is. But these details were obscure to most adults, much less a kid of

Colton's young age. The nature of the Trinity, the role of the Holy Spirit, Jesus sitting at the right hand of God.

I believed. But how could I be sure?

I smoothed Colton's blanket across his chest and tucked him in snug the way he liked—and for the first time since he started talking about heaven, I intentionally tried to trip him up. "I remember you saying you stayed with Pop," I said. "So when it got dark and you went home with Pop, what did you two do?"

Suddenly serious, Colton scowled at me. "It doesn't get dark in heaven, Dad! Who told you *that*?"

I held my ground. "What do you mean it doesn't get dark?"

"God and Jesus light up heaven. It never gets dark. It's always bright."

The joke was on me. Not only had Colton not fallen for the "when it gets dark in heaven" trick, but he could tell me why it didn't get dark: "The city does not need the sun or the moon to shine on it, for the glory of God gives it light, and the Lamb is its lamp."[7]

NINETEEN

JESUS REALLY LOVES THE CHILDREN

For months in late 2003 and early 2004, there was a certain set of things that Colton seemed to fixate on. He talked about death and dying more weird—*really* weird—for a kid his age. He also shared more about what heaven looks like. These details came out in bits and pieces over dinner, while he ran errands with Sonja and me, and during the general flow of life.

He saw the gates of heaven, he said: "They were made of gold and there were pearls on them." The heavenly city itself was made of something shiny, "like gold or silver." The flowers and trees in heaven were "beautiful," and there were animals of every kind.

No matter what new tidbits he revealed, though, Colton had one consistent theme: he talked constantly about how much Jesus loves the children. I mean that: *constantly*.

He would wake up in the morning and tell me: "Hey Dad, Jesus told me to tell you, He really loves the children."

Over dinner at night: "Remember, Jesus really loves the children."

Before bed, as I helped him brush his teeth, "Hey, Daddy don't forget," he'd say, garbling the words through a mouthful of toothpaste foam, "Jesus said he really, *really* loves the children!"

Sonja got the same treatment. She had begun working part-time again by then, and on the days she stayed home with Colton, he chirped all day long about Jesus loving the children. It got so that it didn't matter what Bible story she or I read to our tiny evangelist at night, whether from the Old Testament, the New Testament, about Moses or Noah or King Solomon, Colton wrapped up the night with the same message: "Jesus loves the children!"

Finally I had to tell him, "Colton, we get it. You can stop. When I get to heaven, you are exonerated. I will tell Jesus you did your job."

We might have grown weary of Colton's nonstop message about Jesus' love for kids, but it did transform the way we approached children's ministry in our church. Sonja had always been torn between singing on the worship team during Sunday morning services and going downstairs to teach Sunday school for the kids. And while she knew that statistics show most people who profess faith in Christ do so at a young age, it was Colton's passionate insistence on Christ's love for children that gave Sonja fresh energy for our kids' ministry.

I also became bolder about asking church members to serve in our children's ministry. Over the years, I'd had to fight to get people to sign up to teach Sunday school. They would give me the verbal stiff-arm, saying, "I did my turn last year," or "I'm too old for that."

Now, when I ran into those same excuses, I lovingly reminded people that Jesus clearly viewed children as precious—and that if he loved kids enough to say that adults should be more like them, we should spend more time loving them too.

～

During that time, Colton had also become obsessed with rainbows. All his talk about the magnificent colors in heaven reminded Sonja and me of the book of Revelation, where the apostle John wrote specifically about the rainbow surrounding God's throne,[1] and where he describes heaven as a gleaming city of gold:

> The wall was built of jasper, while the city was pure gold, clear as glass. The foundations of the wall of the city were adorned with every kind of jewel. The first was jasper, the second sapphire, the third agate, the fourth emerald, the fifth onyx, the sixth carnelian, the seventh chrysolite, the eighth beryl, the ninth topaz, the tenth chrysoprase, the eleventh jacinth, the twelfth amethyst.[2]

Some of those precious stones are of colors that are familiar to us: the rich violet of amethyst, the brilliant green of emerald, the translucent gold of topaz, the depthless black of onyx. Others are less common: chrysolite, which is light to olive green; jacinth, a transparent red. Beryl occurs in many colors, from light pink to deep green to aquamarine.

With its unfamiliar gemstones, John's description is so exotic to us that we have to look up the minerals to find out what colors he was talking about; grown-up theologians want to be precise. But if a kid saw all those colors, he might sum them up in one simple word: rainbow.

So when, in the spring of 2004, the most brilliant rainbow we'd ever seen appeared over Imperial, we called him outside to take a look.

Sonja was the first to see it. By then, she was just a few weeks pregnant with the baby we now considered definitively as our *fourth* child. It was a warm, sunny day, and she'd gone to open the front door and let the freshness into the house. "Hey, you guys, come see this!" she called.

From the kitchen, I crossed the dining room to the front door and was astonished to see a rainbow so bright, so vivid, that it looked like an artist's painting of the Perfect Rainbow. Or a kid with a brand-new box of crayons illustrating his science lesson: ROY G BIV. Every color sharply divided from the next, and the whole arc blazing against a perfectly blue sky.

"Did it rain and I missed it?" I asked Sonja.

She laughed. "I don't think so."

Colton was down the hall in the playroom. "Hey, Colton," I called. "Come out and take a look at this."

He emerged from the playroom and joined us on the front stoop.

"Look at that rainbow, Colton," Sonja said. "There definitely should be a big pot of gold at the end of that thing."

Colton squinted, peering up at colors pouring across the sky.

"Cool," he said with a nonchalant smile. "I prayed for that yesterday."

Then he turned on his heel and went back to play.

Sonja and I looked at each other like, *What just happened*? And later we talked again about the pure-faith prayers of a child. "Ask and it will be given to you," Jesus said. He put that instruction in the context of a child asking a father for a blessing.

"Which of you, if his son asks for bread, will give him a stone?" Jesus told the multitudes that gathered to hear his teaching in the low hills of Galilee. "Or if he asks for a fish, will give him a snake? If you, then, though you are evil, know how to give good gifts to your children, how much more will your Father in heaven give good gifts to those who ask him!"[3]

Colton Burpo hadn't seen a rainbow in a while, so he asked his heavenly Father to send one. Faith like a child. Maybe, Sonja and I thought, we had a lot to learn from our son.

TWENTY

DYING AND LIVING

The spring of 2004 marked a year since Colton's hospital stay. That year, Good Friday fell in April, and in just another month, Colton would be five years old. I always enjoyed Good Friday because I'd do what I called a "come-and-go family Communion." That meant that I would hang out at the church for a couple of hours, and families would come and take Communion together. I liked it for a couple of reasons. For one thing, it gave our church families a chance to spend some special time together during Holy Week. Also, it gave me a chance to ask individual families about their prayer needs and pray with the whole family right on the spot.

That morning, I needed to run some errands, so I put Cassie and Colton in my red Chevy truck and drove the few blocks into town. Still small enough to need a booster seat, Colton rode next to me, and Cassie sat by the window. As we drove down Broadway, the main street through town, I was mulling over my responsibilities for the day, thinking ahead to the family Communion service. Then I realized it was a religious holiday and I had a captive audience right there in the truck.

"Hey, Colton, today is Good Friday," I said. "Do you know what Good Friday is?"

Cassie started bouncing up and down on the bench seat and waved her hand in the air like an eager student. "Oh, I know! I know!"

"I don't know," Colton said.

I glanced over at Cassie. "Okay, what's Good Friday?"

"That's the day Jesus died on the cross!"

"Yep, that's right, Cassie. Do you know why Jesus died on the cross?"

At this, she stopped bouncing and started thinking. When she didn't come up with anything right away, I said, "Colton, do you know why Jesus died on the cross?"

He nodded, surprising me a bit.

"Okay, why?"

"Well, Jesus told me he died on the cross so we could go see his Dad."

In my mind's eye, I saw Jesus, with Colton on his lap, brushing past all the seminary degrees, knocking down theological treatises stacked high as skyscrapers, and boiling down fancy words like *propitiation* and *soteriology* to something a child could understand: "I had to die on the cross so that people on earth could come see my Dad."

Colton's answer to my question was the simplest and sweetest declaration of the gospel I had ever heard. I thought again about the difference between grown-up and childlike faith.

Driving down Broadway, I decided I liked Colton's way better. For a couple of minutes, I cruised along in silence. Then I turned to him and smiled. "Hey, do you wanna preach on Sunday?"

~

Later that month, Colton threw me for another loop. This time, it involved life or death.

Sonja and I have a theory: from the time a child walks until about the first grade, one of the main tasks parents have is to keep their kids alive. No forks in the light sockets. No blow-dryers in the bathtub. No soda cans in the microwave. We had done a fine job with Cassie. By then, she was seven years old and had pretty much ceased being a danger to herself and others. Colton, though, was a different story.

As smart as he was about so many things, there was one thing he just couldn't seem to grasp: if a human body meets a moving car, bad things happen.

Even though he was almost ready for kindergarten, he was still a compact little guy, which is a nice way of saying he took after his dad and was short for his age. He was also a ball of fire who, the instant we walked out of a store, would take off running for the car. We were terrified that other drivers wouldn't be able to see him and might back over him. It seemed that at least once or twice a week, we'd have to yank him back from a curb or shout after him, "COLTON, STOP!" then catch up to scold him: "You *have* to wait for us! You *have* to hold Mommy's or Daddy's hand!"

One day in late April, Colton and I had stopped at the Sweden Creme for a snack. The Sweden Creme is the kind of family-owned drive-in joint that is the small-town answer to the fast-food chains that all pass us over because we're too small. Every little town in Nebraska has one of these places. McCook has Mac's; Benkelman has Dub's. In Holyoke, the little burg just over the Colorado state line, it's Dairy King. And they all serve the same thing: hamburger baskets, chicken fingers, and soft-serve ice cream.

That day, I bought vanilla cones, one each for Colton and me. True to form, when we walked out the door, he took his treat and darted out into the parking lot, which is only a couple dozen feet from Broadway.

Heart in my throat, I yelled, "COLTON, STOP!"

He put the brakes on, and I jogged up to him, red in the face, I'm sure. "Son, you *can't do that!*" I said. "How many times have we told you that?"

Just then, I noticed a little pile of fur right out in the middle of Broadway. Seizing what I thought was a teachable moment, I pointed to it. "See that?"

Colton took a lick of his own cone and followed my finger with his eyes.

"That's a bunny who was trying to cross the street and didn't make it," I said. "That's what can happen if you run out and a car doesn't see you! You could not only get hurt; you could die!"

Colton looked up at me and grinned over his cone. "Oh, good!" he said. "That means I get to go back to heaven!"

I just dropped my head and shook it, exasperated. How do you scare some sense into a child who doesn't fear death?

Finally I bent down on one knee and looked at my little boy. "You're missing the point," I said. "This time, I get to heaven first. I'm the dad; you're the kid. Parents go first!"

TWENTY-ONE

THE FIRST PERSON YOU'LL SEE

Most of that summer passed without any new revelations from Colton, though I'm sure we played the "What does Jesus look like?" game on our vacation, with Colton giving a thumbs-down to every picture we saw. It had gotten to the point where instead of asking him, "Is this one right?" Sonja and I had started asking, right off the bat, "So what's wrong with this one?"

August came and with it Imperial's annual claim to fame, the Chase County Fair. Next to the state fair itself, ours is the largest county fair in western Nebraska. In Imperial and the towns for miles around, it is *the* event of the year. For an entire week in late August, Imperial swells from a population of two thousand to somewhere around fifteen thousand. Businesses alter their hours (or shut down entirely), and even the banks close at noon so that the whole community can turn out for concerts (rock on Friday night, country on

Saturday night), vendors, and the spinning rides and lights of a huge carnival midway.

Every year, we look forward to the sights, sounds, and scents of the fair: kettle corn, barbecue, and "Indian tacos" (taco fixings piled on a slab of flatbread). Country music floating out. The Ferris wheel rising above it all, visible from all over town.

This fair is definitely a Midwestern event, with 4-H livestock judging for best bull, best horse, best hog, that kind of thing, along with the kids' favorite: "Mutton Bustin'." In case you've never heard of mutton busting, that's where a child is placed on a sheep and he or she tries to ride it as long as possible without falling off. There's a huge trophy for each age group, five through seven. In fact, the first place trophy is usually taller than the little competitor.

There's definitely a down-home, small-town flavor to our fair, as one lemonade entrepreneur found out the hard way. One year, this gentleman decided he could sell more of his delicious beverage using what you might call the Hooters approach to marketing. After a night or two, a string of folks complained about the scantily clad female sales team in his booth, and a couple of concerned citizens finally had to get on him and tell him the lemonade girls needed to put on more clothes. Still, it seems he did have quite a long line at his stand those first couple of nights.

In August 2004, Sonja and I set up a booth on the midway to interest out-of-town fair visitors in our garage-door business. But as always, I had to carve out time to balance that business with the business of caring for our congregation. One warm afternoon during that fair week, all four of us—Sonja and I and the two kids—were tending the booth, passing out brochures and chatting with prospective customers. But I needed to break away and drive a few blocks over to the Imperial Manor nursing home to visit a man named Harold Greer.

At the time, Harold's daughter, Gloria Marshall, played keyboard on our worship team at church, and her husband, Daniel, was serving as my assistant pastor and worship leader. Harold, himself a minister most of his life, was in his eighties and dying. I knew he was closing in on his last hours and that I needed to pay another visit to support Daniel and Gloria, and to pray with Harold at least one more time.

When you're a pastor/volunteer firefighter/wrestling coach/ business owner trying to juggle all the pins without letting any fall, you learn pretty quickly that children are highly portable. For her part, Sonja was serving as a pastor's wife, a full-time job in itself, plus as a mom, teacher, library volunteer, and secretary for the family business. Over the years, we had developed the habit that if we weren't formally *going to work*, we'd pick a kid and take him or her with us. So that afternoon at the fair, I left Sonja, now seven months pregnant, and Cassie in charge of our vendor booth and strapped Colton into his car seat in my truck, and headed over to the nursing home.

Colton peered out the window as we passed the Ferris wheel on our way off the fairgrounds. "We're going to see Gloria's dad, Harold, at the nursing home," I said. "He's not doing well and probably doesn't have too much time left. Harold gave his life to Jesus a long time ago, and he's getting ready to go to heaven."

Colton didn't look away from the window. "Okay, Daddy."

The nursing home is a sprawling one-story building with a huge dining room off the front lobby, which also houses a giant indoor birdcage filled with finches that flit and tweet and generally bring the outdoors indoors.

When I peeked into Harold's room, I saw Daniel and Gloria, along with three or four family members, including a couple I knew to be Harold's other daughters.

Daniel stood. "Hey, Pastor Todd," he said as I folded his handshake into a hug. Gloria stood, and I hugged her too. The family greeted Colton, who hung onto my hand as he dispensed quiet hellos.

I turned to Harold's bed and saw that he was lying very still, drawing in deep breaths, spaced at wide intervals. I had seen men and women at this phase of the end of life many times. When they reach their last moments, they slip in and out of consciousness and even while awake, in and out of lucidity.

I turned to Gloria. "How's your dad doing?" I asked.

"He's hanging on, but I don't think he has much longer," she said. Her face was brave, but I could see her chin quiver a little as she spoke. Just then, Harold began to moan softly and twist under the thin sheet that covered him. One of Gloria's sisters stood up and walked over to the bed, whispered comforting words, then returned to her seat by the window.

I walked over and stood at Harold's head, Colton trailing me like a tiny shadow. Thin and balding, Harold was lying on his back, his eyes barely open, lips slightly parted. He breathed in through his mouth and seemed to hold it in, as though squeezing every last oxygen molecule from it before exhaling again. I looked down and saw Colton peering up at Harold, a look of utter calm and assurance on his face. I laid my hand on the old minister's shoulder, closed my eyes, and prayed aloud, reminding God of Harold's long and faithful service, asking that the angels would make his journey quick and smooth, and that God would receive his servant with great joy. When I finished the prayer, I turned to rejoin the family. Colton started back across the room with me, but then he spun on his heel and returned to Harold's bedside.

As we watched, Colton reached up and grabbed Harold's hand. It was an E. F. Hutton moment. Everyone watched intently, listening. Colton peered earnestly up into Harold's face and said, "It's going to be okay. The first person you're going to see is Jesus."

His tone was matter-of-fact, as though he were describing something as real and familiar as the town fire station. Daniel and Gloria exchanged looks and a surreal feeling washed over me. By then I was used to hearing Colton talk about heaven. But now he had become a messenger, a tiny tour guide for a departing heavenly traveler.

TWENTY-TWO

NO ONE IS OLD IN HEAVEN

When Pop died in 1975, I inherited a couple of things. I was proud to receive the little .22 rifle I used when he and I hunted prairie dogs and rabbits together. I also inherited Pop's bowling ball and, later, an old desk that my grandpa had had ever since my mom could remember. With a medium stain somewhere between maple and cherry, it was an interesting piece, first because it was a pretty small desk for such a huge man, and second, because the part where you pushed your chair under curved around you instead of being a straight edge like an ordinary desk. When I was a teenager and knee-deep in wood shop at school, I spent many hours in my parents' garage, refinishing Pop's desk. Then I moved it into my room, a sweet reminder of a salt-of-the-earth man.

From the time I put the desk into service, I kept a photo of Pop in the top left drawer and pulled it out every now and then to reminisce. It was the last picture ever taken of my grandfather; it showed him at age sixty-one, with white hair and glasses. When Sonja and I married, the desk and the photo became part of our household.

After Colton started talking about having met Pop in heaven, I noticed that he gave specific physical details about what Jesus looked like, and he also described his unborn sister as "a little smaller than Cassie, with dark hair." But when I asked him what Pop looked like, Colton would talk mainly about his clothes and the size of his wings. When I asked him about facial features, though, he got kind of vague. I have to admit, it was kind of bugging me.

One day not long after our drive to Benkelman, I called Colton down to the basement and pulled my treasured photo of Pop out of the drawer.

"This is how I remember Pop," I said.

Colton took the frame, held it in both hands, and gazed at the photo for a minute or so. I waited for his face to light up in recognition, but it didn't. In fact, a frown crinkled the space between his eyes and he shook his head. "Dad, nobody's old in heaven," Colton said. "And nobody wears glasses."

Then he turned around and marched up the stairs.

Nobody's old in heaven . . .

That statement got me thinking. Sometime later, I called my mom in Ulysses. "Hey, do you have pictures of Pop when he was a young man?"

"I'm sure I do," she said. "I'll have to hunt them down, though. Do you want me to mail them to you?"

"No, I wouldn't want them to get lost. Just make a copy of one and mail that."

Several weeks passed. Then one day, I opened the mailbox

to find an envelope from Mom containing a Xerox copy of an old black-and-white photograph. I learned later that Mom had dug it out of a box that she'd stored in a back bedroom closet since the time Cassie was a baby, a box that hadn't seen daylight since two years before Colton was born.

There were four people in the picture, and Mom had written an accompanying note explaining who they were: My Grandma Ellen, in her twenties in the photo, but now in her eighties and still living in Ulysses. My family had last seen her just a couple of months before. The photo also showed my mom as a baby girl, about eighteen months old; my Uncle Bill, who was about six; and Pop, a handsome fellow, twenty-nine years young when the photo was snapped in 1943.

Of course, I'd never told Colton that it was bugging me that he didn't seem to recognize Pop from my old keepsake photo. That evening, Sonja and I were sitting in the front room when I called Colton to come upstairs. It took him a while to make his appearance, and when he did, I pulled out the photocopied picture Mom had sent.

"Hey, come here and take a look at this, Colton," I said, holding the paper out for him. "What do you think?"

He took the picture from my hand, looked down, and then looked back at me, eyes full of surprise. "Hey!" he said happily. "How did you get a picture of Pop?"

Sonja and I looked at each other, astonished.

"Colton, don't you recognize anyone else in the picture?" I said.

He shook his head slowly. "No . . ."

I leaned over and pointed to my grandma. "Who do you think that is?"

"I don't know."

"That's Grandma Ellen."

Colton's eyes turned skeptical. "That doesn't *look* like Grandma Ellen."

I glanced at Sonja and chuckled. "Well, she used to look like that."

"Can I go play?" Colton said, handing me the picture.

After he left the room, Sonja and I talked about how interesting it was that Colton recognized Pop from a photo taken more than half a century before he was born—a photo he'd never seen before—but didn't recognize his great-grandma whom he had just seen a couple of months back.

After we thought about it, though, the fact that the Pop Colton said he spent time with was no longer sixty-one but somewhere in his prime, seemed to us a good news / bad news scenario: The bad news is that in heaven, we'll still look like ourselves. The good news is, it'll be the younger version.

TWENTY-THREE

POWER FROM ABOVE

On October 4, 2004, Colby Lawrence Burpo entered the world. From the moment he was born, he looked like a carbon copy of Colton. But as with all kids, God had also made him unique. If Cassie was our sensitive child and Colton was our serious one, Colby was our clown. From an early age, Colby's goofiness added a fresh dose of laughter to our home.

One evening later that fall, Sonja had settled in with Colton to read him a Bible story.

She sat on the edge of his bed and read him the story as Colton lay under his blanket, head nestled in his pillow. Then it was time for prayer.

One of the great blessings of our lives as parents has been listening to our kids pray. When they are small, children pray without the showiness that sometimes creeps into our prayers as grown-ups, without that sort of "prayer-ese," a language meant to appeal more to anyone listening than to God. And when Colton and Cassie offered prayers in their plain, earnest way, it seemed that God answered.

Early on, we developed the practice of giving the kids specific things to pray for, not only to build their faith, but also because praying for others is a way to develop a heart for needs outside your own.

"You know how Daddy preaches every week?" Sonja said now as she sat beside Colton. "I think we should pray for him, that he would get a lot of good study time in this week so that he can give a good message in church on Sunday morning."

Colton looked at her and said the strangest thing: "I've seen power shot down to Daddy."

Sonja later told me that she took a moment to turn these words over in her mind. *Power shot down?*

"What do you mean, Colton?"

"Jesus shoots down power for Daddy when he's talking."

Sonja shifted on the bed so that she could look directly into Colton's eyes. "Okay . . . when? Like when Daddy talks at church?"

Colton nodded. "Yeah, at church. When he's telling Bible stories to people."

Sonja didn't know what to say to that, a situation we'd grown used to over the past year and a half. So she and Colton prayed together, sending up flares to heaven that Daddy would give a good message on Sunday.

Then Sonja slipped down the hall to the living room to share their conversation with me. "But don't you dare wake him up to ask him about it!" she said.

So I had to wait until the next morning over breakfast.

"Hey, buddy," I said, pouring milk into Colton's usual bowl of cereal. "Mommy said you were talking last night during Bible story time. Can you tell me what you were telling Mommy about . . . about Jesus shooting down power? What's the power like?"

"It's the Holy Spirit," Colton said simply. "I watched him. He showed me."

"The Holy Spirit?"

"Yeah, he shoots down power for you when you're talking in church."

If there were comic-strip thought-bubbles over people's heads, mine would've been filled with question marks and exclamation points right then. Every Sunday morning before I give the sermon, I pray a similar prayer: "God, if you don't help this morning, this message is going to fail." In light of Colton's words, I realized I had been praying without really knowing what I was praying for. And to imagine God answering it by "shooting down power" . . . well, it was just incredible.

TWENTY-FOUR

ALI'S MOMENT

After Colby was born, Sonja and I had found that the dynamics of taking the kids with us everywhere had changed. Now we were outnumbered three to two. We decided the time had come for a regular babysitter, so we hired a very mature, responsible eighth grader named Ali Titus to watch the kids for us. On Monday nights, Sonja and I still played coed softball on our "old people's" team, though my sliding days were over.

One Monday evening in 2005, Ali came over to babysit Cassie, Colton, and Colby so we could go to our game. It was around 10 p.m. when we pulled back into the driveway. Sonja got out and went inside to check on Ali and the kids while I shut the garage down for the night, so I didn't hear what happened inside until a few minutes after the fact.

The interior garage door leads into our kitchen, and when she walked in, Sonja later told me, she found Ali at the sink, washing up the supper dishes . . . and crying.

"Ali, what's wrong?" Sonja said. Was it something with Ali, or something that had happened with the kids?

Ali pulled her hands from the dishwater and dried them on a towel. "Um . . . I really don't know how to say this, Mrs. Burpo," she began. She looked down at the floor, hesitating.

"It's okay, Ali," Sonja said. "What is it?"

Ali looked up, eyes full of tears. "Well, I'm sorry to ask you this, but . . . did you have a miscarriage?"

"Yes, I did," Sonja said, surprised. "How did you know that?"

"Um . . . Colton and I had a little talk."

Sonja invited Ali to sit on the couch with her and tell her what happened.

"It started after I put Colby and Colton to bed," Ali began. Cassie had gone downstairs to her room, and Ali had given Colby a bottle and then put him down in his crib upstairs. Then she headed down the hall, tucked Colton into his bed, and came out to the kitchen to clean up from the evening meal she'd fed the kids. "I had just turned the water off in the sink when I heard Colton crying."

Ali told Sonja that she went to check on Colton and found him sitting up in his bed, tears streaming down his face. "What's wrong, Colton?" she asked him.

Colton sniffled and wiped his eyes. "I miss my sister," he said.

Ali said she smiled, relieved that the problem seemed to have a simple solution. "Okay, sweetie, you want me to go downstairs and get her for you?"

Colton shook his head. "No, I miss my *other* sister."

Now Ali was confused. "Your other sister? You only have one sister and one brother, Colton. Cassie and Colby, right?"

"No, I have another sister," Colton said. "I saw her. In heaven." Then he started to cry again. "I miss her so much."

As Ali told Sonja this part of the story, her eyes welled with fresh tears. "I didn't know what to say, Mrs. Burpo. He was so upset. So I asked him when he saw this other sister."

Colton told Ali, "When I was little, I had surgery and I went up to heaven and saw my sister."

Then, Ali told Sonja, Colton began crying again, only harder. "I don't understand why my sister is dead," he said. "I don't know why she's in heaven and not here."

Ali sat on the bed beside Colton, as she put it, "in shock." This situation definitely wasn't on the normal "in case of emergency" babysitting list, as in: (1) who to call in case of fire; (2) who to call in case of illness; (3) who to call in case child reports supernatural experience.

Ali knew Colton had been extremely ill a couple of years before and that he'd spent time in the hospital. But she hadn't known about what had happened in the operating room. Now she had no idea what to say, even as Colton shrugged off his covers and crawled up in her lap. So as he cried, she cried with him.

"I miss my sister," he said again, snuffling and laying his head on Ali's shoulder.

"Shh . . . it's okay, Colton," Ali said. "There's a reason for everything." And they stayed that way, with Ali rocking Colton until he cried himself to sleep in her arms.

Ali finished her story, and Sonja gave her a hug. Later, Ali told us that for the next two weeks, she couldn't stop thinking about what Colton had told her, and how Sonja had confirmed that before his surgery, Colton hadn't known anything about Sonja's miscarriage.

Ali had grown up in a Christian home but had entertained the same doubts as so many of us do: for example, how did we know any one religion is different from any other? But Colton's story about his sister strengthened her Christian faith, Ali said. "Hearing him describe the girl's face . . . it wasn't something that a six-year-old boy could just make up," she told us. "Now, whenever I am having doubts, I picture Colton's face, tears running down his cheeks, as he told me how much he missed his sister."

TWENTY-FIVE

SWORDS OF THE ANGELS

From a kid's perspective, maybe the best thing that happened in 2005 was the release of *The Lion, the Witch, and the Wardrobe*. During the Christmas season, we took the kids to see the movie on the big screen. Sonja and I were excited to see the first high-quality dramatization of C. S. Lewis's Chronicles of Narnia series, books we had both enjoyed as kids. Colton was more excited about a movie that featured good guys fighting bad guys with swords.

In early 2006, we rented the DVD and settled into the living room for a family movie night. Instead of sitting on the furniture, we all sat on the carpet, Sonja, Cassie, and I leaning against the sofa. Colton and Colby perched on their knees in front of us, rooting for Aslan, the warrior lion, and the Pevensie kids: Lucy, Edmund, Peter, and Susan. The house even smelled like a theater, with bowls of Act II buttered popcorn, hot out of the microwave, sitting on the floor within easy reach.

In case you haven't seen *The Lion, the Witch, and the Wardrobe*, it is set during World War II when the Pevensie kids are evacuated to London to the home of an eccentric professor. Lucy, Edmund, Peter, and Susan are bored to death, until Lucy stumbles on an enchanted wardrobe that leads into a magical kingdom called Narnia. In Narnia, not only can all the animals talk, but the place is also inhabited by other creatures, like dwarves and centaurs. The land is ruled by the lion Aslan, who is a good and wise king, but his archenemy, the White Witch, has cast a spell on Narnia so that it will always be winter, but never Christmas. Back in the real world, the Pevensies are just kids, but in Narnia, they are kings and queens who also become warriors fighting on the side of Aslan.

That night, as we were watching the final, fantasy / medieval battle scene, Colton, then six, was really getting into it as winged creatures dropped boulders from the sky and the battle-dressed Pevensie kids clashed swords with the White Witch's evil army. Earlier in the film, Aslan had sacrificed himself to save Edmund. But when he came back to life and killed the White Witch, Colton leaped to his feet and pumped his fist. He likes it when the good guys win.

As the credits rolled up the television screen and Colby picked at the dregs of the popcorn, Sonja said offhandedly to Colton, "Well, I guess that's one thing you didn't like about heaven—no swords up there."

Colton's giddy excitement vanished as quickly as if an invisible hand had wiped his smile off with an eraser. He drew himself up to his full height and looked down at Sonja, who was still sitting on the floor.

"There are *too* swords in heaven!" he said.

Surprised at his intensity, Sonja shot me a sideways glance, then kind of drew her head back and smiled at Colton. "Um . . . okay. Why do they need swords in heaven?"

"Mom, Satan's not in hell yet," Colton said, almost scolding. "The angels carry swords so they can keep Satan out of heaven!"

Again, Scripture leaped to my mind, this time from the book of Luke where Jesus tells the disciples, "I saw Satan fall like lightning from heaven."[1]

And I remembered a passage from Daniel in which an angel visits Daniel in answer to prayer, but says he was delayed for twenty-one days because he was engaged in a battle with the "king of Persia."[2] Theologians generally take this to mean some kind of spiritual battle, with Gabriel fighting dark forces.

But how did a six-year-old know that? Yes, Colton had had two more years of Sunday school by then, but I knew for a fact that our curriculum didn't include lessons on Satan's living arrangements.

As these thoughts flashed through my head, I could see that Sonja didn't know what to say to Colton, who was still scowling. His face reminded me of his irritation when I'd suggested that it got dark in heaven. I decided to lighten the mood. "Hey Colton, I bet you asked if you could have a sword, didn't you?" I said.

At that, Colton's scowl melted into a dejected frown, and his shoulders slumped toward the floor. "Yeah, I did. But Jesus wouldn't let me have one. He said I'd be too dangerous."

I chuckled a little, wondering if Jesus meant Colton would be a danger to himself or others.

In all our discussions of heaven, Colton had never mentioned Satan, and neither Sonja nor I had thought to ask
him. When you're thinking "heaven," you're thinking crystal
streams and streets of gold, not angels and demons crossing
swords.

But now that he'd brought it up, I decided to press a little
further.

"Hey, Colton," I said. "Did you *see* Satan?"

"Yeah, I did," he said solemnly.

"What did he look like?"

At this, Colton's body went rigid, he grimaced, and his
eyes narrowed to a squint. He stopped talking. I mean, he
absolutely shut down, and that was it for the night.

We asked Colton about Satan a couple of times after that,
but then gave up because whenever we did, his reaction was
a little disconcerting: it was as if he changed instantly from a
sunny little kid to someone who ran to a safe room, bolted
the door, locked the windows, and pulled down the blinds. It
became clear that in addition to rainbows, horses, and golden
streets, he had seen something unpleasant. And he didn't
want to talk about it.

TWENTY-SIX

THE COMING WAR

A few months later, I had some business in McCook, a town about sixty miles from Imperial and the site of the nearest Wal-Mart. For many Americans, an hour is an awfully long way to drive to get to Wal-Mart, but out here in farm country, you get used to it. I had taken Colton with me, and I'll never forget the conversation we had on the way back, because while our son had spoken to me about heaven and even about my own past, he had never before hinted that he knew my future.

We had driven back through Culbertson, the first town west of McCook, and were passing a cemetery. Colton, by now out of a car seat, gazed out the passenger-side window as the rows of headstones filed past.

"Dad, where's Pop buried?" he asked

"Well, his body is buried in a cemetery down in Ulysses, Kansas, where Grandma Kay lives," I said. "Next time we're down there, I can take you to see where it is if you want. But you know that's not where Pop is."

Colton kept peering out the window. "I know. He's in heaven. He's got a new body. Jesus told me if you don't go to heaven, you don't get a new body."

Hang on, I thought. *New information ahead.*

"Really?" was all I said.

"Yeah," he said, then added, "Dad, did you know there's going to be a war?"

"What do you mean?" Were we still on the heaven topic? I wasn't sure.

"There's going to be a war, and it's going to destroy this world. Jesus and the angels and the good people are going to fight against Satan and the monsters and the bad people. I saw it."

I thought of the battle described in the book of Revelation, and my heartbeat stepped up a notch. "How did you see that?"

"In heaven, the women and the children got to stand back and watch. So I stood back and watched." Strangely, his voice was sort of cheerful, as though he were talking about a good movie he'd seen. "But the men, they had to fight. And Dad, I watched you. You have to fight too."

Try hearing that and staying on the road. Suddenly, the sound of the tires whirring on asphalt seemed unnaturally loud, a high whine.

And here was this issue of "heaven time" again. Before, Colton had talked about my past, and he had seen "dead" people in the present. Now he was saying that in the midst of all that, he had also been shown the future. I wondered if those concepts—past, present, and future—were for earth only. Maybe, in heaven, time isn't linear.

But I had another, more pressing concern. "You said we're fighting monsters?"

"Yeah," Colton said happily. "Like dragons and stuff."

I'm not one of those preachers who camps out on end-times prophecy, but now I remembered a particularly vivid section of Revelation:

> In those days men will seek death and will not find it; they will desire to die, and death will flee from them. The shape of the locusts was like horses prepared for battle. On their heads were crowns of something like gold, and their faces were like the faces of men. They had hair like women's hair, and their teeth were like lions' teeth. And they had breastplates like breastplates of iron, and the sound of their wings was like the sound of chariots with many horses running into battle. They had tails like scorpions, and there were stings in their tails. Their power was to hurt men five months.[1]

For centuries, theologians have mined these kinds of passages for symbolism: maybe the combination of all those different body parts stood for some kind of country, or each one stood for a kingdom of some sort. Others have suggested that "breastplates of iron" indicate some kind of modern military machine that John had no reference point to describe.

But maybe we sophisticated grown-ups have tried to make things more complicated than they are. Maybe we are too educated, too "smart," to name these creatures in the simple language of a child: monsters.

"Um, Colton . . . what am I fighting the monsters with?" I was hoping for a tank, maybe, or a missile launcher . . . I didn't know, but something I could use to fight from a distance.

Colton looked at me and smiled. "You either get a sword or a bow and arrow, but I don't remember which."

My face fell. "You mean I have to fight monsters with a *sword*?"

"Yeah, Dad, but it's okay," he said reassuringly. "Jesus wins. He throws Satan into hell. I saw it."

And I saw an angel come down from heaven, having the key of the bottomless pit and a great chain in his hand. And he laid hold on the dragon, that old serpent, which is the Devil, and Satan, and bound him a thousand years, And cast him into the bottomless pit, and shut him up, and set a seal upon him, that he should deceive the nations no more, till the thousand years should be fulfilled: and after that he must be loosed a little season. . . . And when the thousand years are expired, Satan shall be loosed out of his prison, And shall go out to deceive the nations which are in the four quarters of the earth, Gog and Magog, to gather them together to battle: the number of whom is as the sand of the sea. And they went up on the breadth of the earth, and compassed the camp of the saints about, and the beloved city: and fire came down from God out of heaven, and devoured them. And the devil that deceived them was cast into the lake of fire and brimstone, where the beast and the false prophet are, and shall be tormented day and night for ever and ever.[2]

Colton was describing the battle of Armageddon and saying I was going to fight in it. For the umpteenth time in the
nearly two years since Colton first told us the angels sang to
him at the hospital, my head was spinning. I drove on, speechless, for several miles as I kicked around these new images in
my head. Also, Colton's nonchalance struck me. His attitude
was kind of like, "What's the problem, Dad? I've told you:
I've skipped to the last chapter, and the good guys win."

That was some comfort at least. We were just crossing the
outskirts of Imperial when I decided to adopt his attitude
toward the whole thing. "Well, son, I guess if Jesus wants me
to fight, I'll fight," I said.

Colton turned away from the window, and I saw that the
look on his face had turned serious. "Yeah, I know, Dad," he
said. "You will."

TWENTY-SEVEN

SOMEDAY WE'LL SEE

I remember the first time we spoke publicly about Colton's experience. It was during the evening service on January 28, 2007, at Mountain View Wesleyan Church in Colorado Springs. During the morning service, I preached the sermon, a message about Thomas, the disciple who was angry because the other disciples, and even Mary Magdalene, had gotten to see the risen Christ and he hadn't. The story is told in the gospel of John:

> Now Thomas (called Didymus), one of the Twelve, was not with the disciples when Jesus came. So the other disciples told him, "We have seen the Lord!"
>
> But he said to them, "Unless I see the nail marks in his hands and put my finger where the nails were, and put my hand into his side, I will not believe it."
>
> A week later his disciples were in the house again, and Thomas was with them. Though the doors were locked, Jesus came and stood among them and said, "Peace be with you!" Then he said to Thomas, "Put your finger here; see

my hands. Reach out your hand and put it into my side. Stop doubting and believe."

Thomas said to him, "My Lord and my God!"

Then Jesus told him, "Because you have seen me, you have believed; blessed are those who have not seen and yet have believed."[1]

This story is where we get the familiar term "doubting Thomas," someone who refuses to believe something without physical evidence or direct personal experience. In other words, a person without faith.

In my sermon that morning, I talked about my own anger and lack of faith, about the stormy moments I spent in that little room in the hospital, raging against God, and about how God came back to me, through my son, saying, *"Here I am."*

People who attended the service that morning went out and told their friends that a preacher and his wife whose son had been to heaven would be telling more of the story during the evening service. That night, the church was packed. Colton, by now seven years old, sat in the second pew along with his brother and sister while Sonja and I told the story of his experience as well as we could in the space of forty-five minutes. We shared about Pop, and Colton's meeting his unborn sister; then we answered questions for a good forty-five minutes after that.

About a week after we got back to Imperial, I was down in my basement office at home, checking e-mail, when I saw one from the family at whose home Sonja and I and the kids had stayed during our visit to Mountain View Wesleyan. Our

hosts had friends who had been at the church the evening of
our talk and had heard the descriptions of heaven Colton had
shared. Via our hosts, those friends had forwarded us an
e-mail about a report CNN had run just two months earlier,
in December 2006. The story was about a young Lithuanian-
American girl named Akiane Kramarik, who lived in Idaho.
Twelve years old at the time of the CNN segment, Akiane
(pronounced AH-KEE-AHNA) had begun having "visions"
of heaven at the age of four, the e-mail said. Her descriptions
of heaven sounded remarkably like Colton's, and our host's
friends thought we'd be interested in the report.

Sitting at the computer, I clicked on the link to the three-
minute segment that began with background music, a slow
classical piece on cello. A male voice-over said: "A self-taught
artist who says her inspiration comes 'from above.' Paintings
that are spiritual, emotional . . . and created by a twelve-year-
old prodigy."[2]

Prodigy was right. As the cello played, the video showed
painting after painting of angelic-looking figures, idyllic
landscapes, and a profile view of a man who was clearly
meant to be Christ. Then a shot of a young girl filling a
canvas with color. But these didn't seem to be paintings by
a young girl, or even of an adult learning to paint portraits.
This was sophisticated artwork that could hang in any
gallery.

Akiane began painting at the age of six, the voice-over
said, but at age four she "began to describe to her mother her
visits to heaven."

Then Akiane spoke for the first time: "All the colors were

out of this world," she said, describing heaven. "There are hundreds of millions of more colors we don't know yet."

The narrator went on to say that Akiane's mother was an atheist and that the concept of God was never discussed in their home. The family did not watch television, and Akiane didn't attend any kind of preschool. So as the little girl began to tell her stories of heaven, then depict them first in drawings, then paintings, her mother knew she couldn't have heard these things from another person. Slowly, her mom began to accept that Akiane's visions were real and that therefore, God must be real.

"I think that God knows where he puts our children, in each family," Mrs. Kramarik said.

I remembered what Jesus told his disciples one day when they were trying to keep some kids from "bothering" him: "Let the little children come to me."[3]

I made a mental note for future sermons: Akiane's story showed that God can reach anyone, anywhere, at any age— even a preschool girl in a home where his name had never been spoken.

But that was not the lesson God had for me that day.

As I watched a montage of Akiane's artwork play across my computer screen, the narrator said, "Akiane describes God as vividly as she paints him."

At that point, a close-up portrait of the face of Christ filled the screen. It was the same likeness I'd seen before, but this time with Jesus looking directly "into the camera," so to speak.

"He's pure," Akiane was saying. "He's very masculine, really strong and big. And his eyes are just beautiful."

Wow. Nearly three years had passed since Colton's surgery, and about two and a half years since he first described Jesus to me that night in the basement. I was struck by the similarities between his and Akiane's recollections: all the colors in heaven . . . and especially their descriptions of Jesus' eyes.

"And his eyes," Colton had said. "Oh, Dad, his eyes are *so* pretty!"

What an interesting detail for two four-year-olds to key in on. After the CNN report concluded, I rewound it to that second portrait of Jesus, a startlingly realistic picture that Akiane painted when she was eight. The eyes were indeed striking—a clear, greenish blue under bold, dark brows—with half the face in shadow. And I noticed that his hair was shorter than most artists paint it. The beard was also different, fuller somehow, more . . . I don't know . . . casual.

Still, of the literally dozens of portraits of Jesus we'd seen since 2003, Colton had still never seen one he thought was right.

Well, I thought, *may as well see what he thinks of Akiane's attempt.*

I got up from the desk and hollered up the stairs for Colton to come down to the basement.

"Coming!" came the reply.

Colton bounded down the stairs and popped into the office. "Yeah, Dad?"

"Take a look at this," I said, nodding toward the computer monitor. "What's wrong with this one?"

He turned to the screen and for a long moment said nothing.

"Colton?"

But he just stood there, studying. I couldn't read his expression.

"What's wrong with this one, Colton?" I said again.

Utter silence.

I nudged him in the arm. "Colton?"

My seven-year-old turned to look at me and said, "Dad, that one's right."

~

Knowing how many pictures Colton had rejected, Sonja and I finally felt that in Akiane's portrait, we'd seen the face of Jesus. Or at least a startling likeness.

We were pretty sure no painting could ever capture the majesty of the person of the risen Christ. But after three years of examining Jesus pictures, we did know that Akiane's rendering was not only a departure from typical paintings of Jesus; it was also the only one that had ever stopped Colton in his tracks. Sonja and I thought it was interesting that when Colton said, "This one's right," he hadn't known the portrait, called *Prince of Peace: The Resurrection*, was painted by another child—a child who had also claimed to visit heaven.

Finally getting an idea of what Jesus looks like wasn't the only interesting thing that came out of our visit to Mountain View Wesleyan. It was also the first time we realized how Colton's encounter with his sister in heaven would impact people on earth.

After the service that evening in January 2007, a young mother came up to me, her eyes brimming with tears.

"I lost a baby," she said. "She was stillborn. Would your son know if my baby's in heaven?"

The woman's voice trembled, and I saw that she was physically shaking. I thought, *Oh, Lord, who am I to answer this question?*

Colton had said there were many, many children in heaven. But it wasn't like I could go and ask him if he'd seen this woman's particular child. Still, I didn't want to just leave her hanging in her grief either.

Just then, a little boy of about six or seven came and stood beside the woman, clinging to her skirt. And an answer came to me.

"Ma'am, do you believe God loves me?" I said.

She blinked away her tears. "Well . . . yes."

"Do you believe he loves you as much as he loves me?"

"Yes. Yes, I do."

Then I nodded at her young son beside her. "Do you believe God loves your son here as much as he loves Colton?"

She paused to process that question, then answered, "Yes, of course."

"Well, if you believe God loves you as much as he loves me, and you believe he loves your living son as much as he loves my living son, don't you believe he loves your unborn child as much as he loves mine?"

Suddenly, the woman stopped trembling and smiled. "I never thought about it that way."

I breathed a prayer of thanks to the Holy Spirit, who had clearly "shot down power," giving me an answer for this grieving woman, because I can tell you right now, I'm not smart enough to have thought of it myself.

That wouldn't be the last time Colton's story put me or Sonja in the position of trying to answer some monumental questions. But sometimes, people who walked through the experience with us have had some questions answered for themselves.

As I mentioned earlier, before we were released from the hospital in North Platte, nurses kept filing in and out of Colton's room. Before, when nurses visited our room, they'd check Colton's vitals and write stuff on charts. Now they came with no medical business whatsoever—just stole glances at this little guy who, only two days before, was beyond their medical capabilities but who now was up in his bed, chattering and playing with his new stuffed lion. During that time, one of the nurses pulled me aside. "Mr. Burpo, can I speak with you for a moment?"

"Sure," I said.

She indicated a room across the hall from Colton's room. "Let's step in here."

Wondering what was up, I followed her into what appeared to be a small break room. She closed the door behind us and turned to face me. Her eyes held a deep sparkle, as though something new had just blossomed inside her.

"Mr. Burpo, I've worked as a nurse here for many years," she said. "I'm not supposed to tell you this, but we were told not to give your family any encouragement. They didn't think Colton was going to make it. And when they tell us people aren't going to make it, they don't."

She seemed to hesitate for a moment; then she plunged on. "But seeing your boy the way he is today, this is a miracle. There has to be a God, because this is a miracle."

I thanked her for sharing with me, then said, "I want you to know that we believe this was God. Our church got together and prayed for Colton last night, and we believe God answered our prayers."

The nurse looked at the floor for a moment, then back up at me again and smiled. "Well, I just wanted to tell you that."

Then she left. I think maybe she didn't want to hear a sermon from a pastor. But the truth was, she didn't need a sermon—she'd already seen one.

Speaking of Colton's experience in heaven, people have said to us, "Your family is so blessed!"

In the sense that we've had a glimpse through the veil that separates earth from eternity, they're right.

But I also think, *Blessed? We watched our son almost die.*

It's fun to talk about heaven, about the throne of God and Jesus and Pop and the daughter we thought we had lost but will meet again someday. But it's not fun to talk about how we got there. Recalling those terrifying days when we watched Colton cling to life still brings tears for Sonja and me. To this day, the miraculous story of his visit to heaven and the story of almost losing our son are one and the same event to us.

When I was a kid, I always wondered why the cross, Jesus' crucifixion, was such a big deal. If God the Father knew he was going to raise his Son from the dead, how was that a sacrifice? But now I understand why God doesn't view Easter as just the endgame, just the empty tomb. I understand completely. I would've done anything, *anything*, to stop Colton's suffering, including trading places with him.

The Scripture says that as Jesus gave up his spirit, as he sagged there, lifeless on that Roman cross, God the Father turned his back. I am convinced that he did that because if he had kept on watching, he couldn't have gone through with it.

Sometimes people ask, "Why Colton? Why do you think this happened to your family?" I've had to say on more than one occasion, "Hey, we're just ordinary people from a one-horse town in Nebraska. The best we can do is tell you what happened to us, and hope that you find it encouraging, like the nurse in North Platte who maybe needed to see a miracle to believe there is Someone greater than ourselves. Or the woman at Mountain View Wesleyan who needed a glimmer of hope to help her cope with her grief. Or Sonja, who needed salve on her own maternal wounds. Or like my mother, Kay, who after twenty-eight years of wondering, finally knows she will one day meet her father again."

When you look at the book of Revelation and other biblical teachings about heaven, it's kind of fragmented. As a pastor, I've always been very conscious about what I share about heaven from the pulpit, and I still am. I teach what I find in Scripture.

Because I had a lot of questions that I didn't have answers for, I didn't spend much time thinking about heaven on a personal level. But I do now. Sonja and I both do, and we've heard from a lot of people that Colton's story has them thinking more about heaven too. We still don't have all the answers—not even close. But now we have a picture in our minds, a picture we can look at and say, "Wow."

I love the way my mom sums it up: "Ever since this happened," she told me, "I think more about what it might really be like in heaven. I accepted the idea of heaven before, but now I visualize it. Before, I'd heard, but now I know that someday I'm going to see."

EPILOGUE

Just over seven years have passed since an ordinary family trip turned into a heavenly trip that changed all our lives. People have often asked us why we waited so long to tell Colton's story. Well, there are a couple of reasons. First, though it's been seven years since the hospital ordeal, our emergency dash from Greeley to the doctor in Imperial turned out to be only the beginning of the story. As you've read in these pages, we received the details of Colton's extraordinary journey in bits and pieces over a period of months and years. So though it's been some time since his brush with death, the rest of the story took a while to unfold.

Then, when we began to share with others what had happened, many people told us, "You should write a book!" to which Sonja and I responded, "Us? Write a book? Yeah, right."

For one thing, we couldn't get our head around the idea that anyone would want to read about *us*. Then there was the whole writing-a-book thing itself. That sounded to us about a notch lower on the huge-undertaking scale than flying to the moon. Sure, I edited my college newspaper, and Sonja wrote a lot in pursuit of her master's degree. But we both had jobs we loved, young children to raise, and a church to care for. And you have to sleep sometime. It was only after Phil McCallum, a pastor friend, offered to make some introductions and get the right publishing people around us that we thought we might actually be able to make a book happen. Even that, though, was a matter of timing.

See, as parents we were concerned about Colton. A lot of people love his story because of all the details about heaven. We like that too. But then there's that hospital part when we all walked through terror and misery for what seemed an eternity. That was still tender territory and we weren't sure how reliving it all would affect Colton. Also, how would he handle the attention? We were concerned about that. We're still concerned. We're from small towns, small schools, small churches. "Small" is something Colton knows, but the spotlight? We're not so sure.

But now, of course, the book is written. Sonja said to me the other day, laughing, "Well, I guess we'll have to write 'become author' on our bucket lists just so we can cross it off."

People have asked us other questions as well. Kids, especially, want to know whether Colton saw any animals in heaven. The answer is yes! Besides Jesus' horse, he told us he saw dogs, birds, even a lion—and the lion was friendly, not fierce.

A lot of our Catholic friends have asked whether Colton saw Mary, the mother of Jesus. The answer to that is also yes. He saw Mary kneeling before the throne of God and at other times, standing beside Jesus. "She still loves him like a mom," Colton said.

Another question people ask all the time is how Colton's experience has changed us. The first thing Sonja will tell you is that it absolutely broke us. See, pastors and their families are usually most comfortable in the role of "helper," not "helpee." Sonja and I had always been the ones who visited the sick, brought the meals, cared for others' kids, in times of need. We were adamantly self-reliant—maybe, in retrospect, to the point of being prideful. But that grueling stint in the hospital snapped our pride like a dry twig and taught us how to be humble enough to accept help from other people, physically, emotionally, and financially.

It's good to be strong and able to bless others, yes. But we learned the value of being vulnerable enough to let others be strong for us, to let others bless us. That, it turned out, was a blessing to them as well.

Another way Colton's story has changed us is this: we are bolder. We live in a day and time when people question the existence of God. As a pastor, I was always comfortable talking about my faith, but now, in addition, I talk about what happened to my son. It's the truth and I talk about it, no apologies.

Meanwhile, here in Imperial, the business of living goes on just the same as it does for families all across small-town America. Cassie is thirteen and headed for high school in the fall. Last night was a big night for her: she tried out for the high school show choir. Our youngest, Colby, is also reaching a milestone: He's starting kindergarten this year, which is a good thing because he was starting to drive his preschool teacher nuts.

As for Colton, he'll turn eleven this month and in September will enter the sixth grade. He's a regular kid in every way. He wrestles and plays baseball. He plays the piano and the trumpet, but isn't too wild about school and says his favorite subject is recess. He still talks about heaven occasionally, but he hasn't claimed to have gone on any more trips or to have any kind of special, ongoing connection with eternity. And despite his supernatural journey, his relationships with his siblings are as natural as can be. Colby follows Colton around little-brother-style, and they fight over who stole whose action figures. Cassie, meanwhile, is the long-suffering older sister. This was demonstrated perfectly when we were all trying to think up a good title for this book.

I suggested *Heaven by Four*.

Sonja suggested *Heaven, According to Colton*.

Cassie suggested *He's Back, but He's No Angel*.

In the end, though, it was Colton who inadvertently came up with the title. Around Christmastime in 2009, we had taken a family trip down to Texas and were sitting with our editor at a Starbucks in Dallas, discussing the book. She looked across the table at our oldest son and said, "Colton, what do *you* want people to know from your story?"

Without hesitation, he looked her in the eye and said, "I want them to know that heaven is for real."

Todd Burpo
Imperial, Nebraska
May 2010

TIMELINE OF EVENTS

July 1976—Todd Burpo's grandpa, whom he calls "Pop" (Lawrence Edelbert Barber), dies in a car accident between Ulysses and Liberal, Kansas.

1982—Todd as a thirteen-year-old hears and accepts Christ's call into ministry as a preacher of the gospel.

December 29, 1990—Todd and Sonja Burpo are married.

August 16, 1996—Cassie Burpo, Colton's older sister, is born.

July 1997—Pastor Todd and Sonja Burpo accept a call to the Crossroads Wesleyan Church in Imperial, Nebraska.

June 20, 1998—Sonja Burpo miscarries their second child. She is two months along.

May 19, 1999—Colton Burpo is born.

August 2002—Todd shatters his leg in a coed softball tournament game.

October 2002—Todd develops kidney stones.

November 2002—Todd feels a lump in his chest that is diagnosed as hyperplasia.

February 27, 2003—Colton complains of stomach pain and has a high fever that is misdiagnosed as stomach flu.

February 28, 2003—Colton's fever breaks. His parents rejoice, thinking that Colton is well, when in fact this is a sign of the rupturing of his appendix.

March 1, 2003—The Burpo family visits the Denver Butterfly Pavilion to celebrate Todd's recovery. That night Colton begins vomiting uncontrollably.

March 3, 2003—Colton is examined by a doctor in Imperial, Nebraska, who dismisses suggestions of appendicitis.

March 5, 2003—Todd and Sonja personally check Colton out of the Imperial, Nebraska, hospital and take their son by car to North Platte, Nebraska's Great Plains Regional Medical Center. Dr. Timothy O'Holleran prepares for surgery.

March 5, 2003—Colton undergoes his first surgery, an appendectomy. He has both a ruptured appendix and an abscess.

March 13, 2003—Colton is discharged from the hospital. But as Todd and Sonja wheel him into the elevator, Dr. O'Holleran shouts down the hallway for them to return. Blood tests reveal Colton's white blood cell count has spiked. A CT scan reveals two more abscesses in his abdomen.

March 13, 2003—Colton undergoes a second surgery—a celiotomy—to drain the abscess. During surgery a total of three abscesses are found.

March 17, 2003—Dr. O'Holleran advises Todd and Sonja that there is nothing more he can do for Colton. He recommends that Colton be transferred to the Denver Children's Hospital. A blizzard blocks all exits with two feet of snow. Back home in Imperial, their congregation gathers for a prayer meeting.

March 18, 2003—The next morning, Colton shows amazing signs of recovery and is soon playing like a normal kid. He skips to his CT scan, which shows no more obstruction.

March 19, 2003—After seventeen harrowing days, Colton's family returns to Imperial.

July 3, 2003—While en route to visit his cousin in South Dakota, Colton tells the first of many accounts of heaven while parked in an Arby's parking lot in North Platte, Nebraska. Colton progressively tells more stories of his adventures in heaven.

October 4, 2004—Colby Burpo, Colton's younger brother, is born.

May 19, 2010—Colton Burpo turns eleven. He remains physically healthy.

NOTES

Chapter 2: *Pastor Job*
   1. Matthew 10:24.

Chapter 6: *North Platte*
   1. 2 Samuel 12:13–14, paraphrased.
   2. 2 Samuel 12:21–23, paraphrased.

Chapter 9: *Minutes Like Glaciers*
   1. Matthew 9:6.

Chapter 12: *Eyewitness to Heaven*
   1. Mark 9:3.
   2. Revelation 21:19–20.

Chapter 13: *Lights and Wings*
   1. Acts 1:9–11.
   2. Matthew 28:3.
   3. Acts 6:15 NLT.
   4. Revelation 10:1 NLT.
   5. Matthew 18:3–4.
   6. Daniel 10:4–6.

Chapter 14: *On Heaven Time*
   1. 2 Peter 3:8.
   2. 2 Corinthians 12:2–4.
   3. Revelation 4:1–3.

Chapter 18: The Throne Room of God
1. Hebrews 4:16.
2. Hebrews 12:2.
3. Revelation 21:2–5a, 22–23.
4. Hebrews 12:2.
5. Luke 1:13–15a, 18–19.
6. Hebrews 12:1.
7. Revelation 21:23.

Chapter 19: Jesus Really Loves the Children
1. Revelation 4:3.
2. Revelation 21:18–20 ESV.
3. Matthew 7:7, 9–11.

Chapter 25: Swords of the Angels
1. Luke 10:18.
2. Daniel 10:13.

Chapter 26: The Coming War
1. Revelation 9:6–10 NKJV.
2. Revelation 20:1–3, 7–10 KJV.

Chapter 27: Someday We'll See
1. John 20:24–29.
2. Akiane Kramarik, *Akiane: Her Life, Her Art, Her Poetry* (Nashville: Thomas Nelson, 2006).
3. Mark 10:14.

Heaven Is for Real

CONVERSATION GUIDE

Introduction

Get up early. Take care of the kids. Go to work. Find something for dinner. Get ready for tomorrow. This is real life; and we know all about real life, as we face it and its trials with each new day. We know the face of death, too: cancer, heart attacks, car accidents, illness—it's all too real.

But what happens after that final earthly breath? How can we know what waits on the other side? What does our existence look like in the world beyond the only one we know?

Death is a mystery for all. For those who don't know Jesus, the thought of death can be terrifying. Christians around the world know we have the eternal home of heaven waiting for us. But death remains mysterious, and the unknown can bring fear in its wake, even for those whose faith in Jesus Christ gives them assurance of life after death.

Through *Heaven Is for Real*, you shared Colton's miraculous glimpse of the world that awaits us when our time on this earth is done. This study guide will lead you, together with your small group, on an even more dynamic and candid journey with our family—a journey that will allow you to experience through Colton's eyes and apprehend through God's Word the truth regarding eternity and what it holds for those who know Jesus.

Colton chose the name for his book; he wants everyone to know that heaven is definitely "for real." He wants all to discover the truth in Jesus' words, "For God so loved the world that He gave His only begotten Son, that whoever believes in Him should not perish but have everlasting life. For God did not send His Son into the world to condemn the world, but that the world through Him might be saved. He who believes in Him is not condemned; but he who does not believe is condemned already, because he has not believed in the name of the only begotten Son of God" (John 3:16–18 NKJV).

For those who do not know Jesus as their Savior, this study will act as a guide to Jesus—the Way, the Truth, and the Life—and will help you learn how you can experience the kingdom of God both today and eternally. For Christians, this guide is a call to share what we know is true, to put uncertainty behind us, and to let others know and rest assured that heaven is a real place that awaits those who have made Jesus Christ their Savior and Lord.

The *Heaven Is for Real* Group Experience

This study is based on Colton's story and our family's experiences since we shared Colton's tour of heaven with the world. Its purpose is to strengthen those who already know the

Lord and to enlighten those who do not. We will discuss many aspects of our family's experience, going to the Word of God as the final authority. We hope you find the time you spend exploring the biblical foundations of *Heaven Is for Real* with your small group to be encouraging, challenging, and life changing.

Your small group is an expression of the body of Christ in action. Each member has a unique view and a necessary voice. To encourage candid and open participation in this group, we want to create an environment in which everyone is valued equally, regardless of his or her spiritual faith definition; and where all are encouraged share freely, question, and comment without fear or hesitation. All are encouraged to be authentic and transparent and to participate to the degree that they are able. To this end, we need to realize that compassion and respect are key elements of small group life. These are lived out through listening to one another, praying for and encouraging one another, and holding in strict confidence anything of a personal nature shared within your group. Criticizing or condemning one another will only serve to discourage sharing and limit your small group experience.

Remember, as with most things in life, you will get as much from this study as you are willing to give. Approach it with an open mind. Set aside the time with your small group to grow closer to the Lord and receive from His Spirit. Take time throughout the week to read God's Word and discover for yourself the revelations regarding the abundant life available in God's kingdom today and His eternal promises for the world to come. Pray diligently for the people in your small group, and celebrate together as you watch the Holy Spirit "shoot down power" to transform circumstances, change hearts, and heal lives.

Now let's join our hearts and minds together as we learn more about eternity and how to walk in powerful, childlike, confident faith.

How to Use This Guide

The reaction to Colton's story as told in *Heaven Is for Real* has been extraordinary. For some the book has been a tremendous encouragement and source of healing; for others, it has been a source of confusion and animosity. We felt strongly that we should address those concerns as well as provide greater insight into our experiences and the biblical foundations of our message. *Heaven Is for Real* is the story; this study will take you beyond the story into the kingdom dynamics and biblical truth surrounding Colton's experiences in heaven and our family's experiences since our story became known.

DVD

During your small group time, you will watch a DVD together that will address different aspects of Colton's experience and the issues that have arisen since his time in heaven. Each DVD session is divided into two sections: an introductory message and an interview with Colton and our family. Although it is not necessary to read *Heaven Is for Real* before you walk with us through this study, we strongly encourage you to read it first in order to better relate to the events discussed in the video.

DISCUSSION

So many questions exist in all our minds regarding death. You may simply want to face this issue in light of biblical truth; maybe you find the reality of your own death to be a fearful one; or possibly the death of a loved one has left you with a broken heart or empty arms. Regardless of the reason you chose to begin this journey, your small group can be a source of support and encouragement.

We chose to format this study for a small group in order to provide an atmosphere of community—a "mini body of Christ," so to speak. As the apostle Paul said, "For as we have many members in one body, but all the members do not have the same function, so we, being many, are one body in Christ, and individually members of one another" (Romans 12:4–5 NKJV).

Your group is made up of people who desire to know more about the Lord and His kingdom. It is a safe place to share your questions, concerns, sorrows, and pain. As you share openly and allow others to explore their own thoughts and feelings as you discover truth together, all will be strengthened.

For each session of this study, we have provided discussion questions or topics to enhance your experience. These should be considered discussion starters, not a road map. Don't be concerned if all the questions for each session are not addressed. The important thing in this study is real, authentic, open, and honest sharing. When seekers and believers operate in love, compassion, and honesty, the power of the Holy Spirit will lead all to the truth. Dare to be transparent; take a chance on your group, and be a willing vessel of love and compassion. You will find the reward is well worth the risk.

REAL REFLECTIONS

After each session, you will find a personal devotion section titled "Real Reflection." This portion of the guide is designed to help you dig deeper into God's Word and further develop your relationship with our Lord. You will be presented with further Scripture reading and devotional or inspirational topics to encourage and solidify your faith. Personal time with the Lord is critical to a life of faith. We strongly encourage you to set aside time each day to talk to God, read His Word, and bask in the love that flows from Him toward you. As Colton says, "He really, really loves us . . . You can't *belieeeve* how much he loves us!"

JOURNAL

During our time together, we will examine many issues that will touch our lives and impact our hearts deeply. We will spend quality time together each week; but hopefully, we will each spend some very intimate, quality time thinking about our time together and prayerfully asking Jesus to give us understanding and faith. Whenever we take time to truly consider the truth of God's Word, Jesus will speak to our hearts and minds. Although space has been provided in this guide to record your thoughts, you may find a notebook to be valuable, especially as you spend time with the Lord during your Real Reflections each week. You will not be required to share what you write in your journal, though you may if you choose. So you can feel totally free to write out your questions, put your feelings into words, and record the truth you discover as you seek the Lord and listen for His voice.

BRINGING IT HOME

As you walk through this time with your small group, the insights you gain will be life changing. You may wish to share your experience with your family. In order to equip you to include your family in your journey, we have included family discussion topics and questions at the end of each session. You can tailor these suggestions to fit your own family dynamics and personality.

Our family has experienced together the encouragement and hope generated by Colton's trip to heaven. It is our desire that you and your family experience the wonder, peace, and lifelong hope in knowing that *heaven is for real.*

Why Should We Care About Heaven?

Colton knows for certain that heaven is for real, and so do we. We are an ordinary family in the midst of extraordinary circumstances, desiring to be faithful to God and to be a source of encouragement to those who encounter us and our story. The message of the reality of heaven we've been given to share is serious and powerful because it deals with eternal truth. It is a message of hope and peace. The world is full of seekers desperately trying to find truth, hope, and peace. God can use Colton's journey to speak directly to those needs. We pray that the clarity of his four-year-old's description of our eternal home can cut through the confusions of this world, wherever they are found, even in the minds and spirits of those who are already believers in Jesus Christ.

We have discovered that our family is not alone. All over the body of Christ, we have found people who identify with our experiences and who are encouraging one another and building one another up in the faith (see 1 Thessalonians 5:11).

But whenever a message is shared, there will always be skeptics. In view of the importance of this message, careful, open-minded consideration is wise. Some people are determined not to believe, no matter what the evidence. It's not for us to argue and convince. It is for us to share this reality as faithfully as we can, just as it is every Christian's job to share the realities of Christ and our eternal home. We pray that our journey will be a strong witness to those who don't believe, but also be a strengthening balm to those who do.

We have seen the power of the Word of God in our lives. Colton's experience has only strengthened our faith in God's Word and its unalterable truth. It is powerful and relevant to our lives today, and for eternity. So now we want to spend time in Scripture, our final authority, to explore why we should care about heaven.

Group Discussion

Why did you decide to participate in this study?

❋ Is the reality of heaven something you have ever thought or cared about before today? Why or why not?

❋ Do you believe we will experience an afterlife? If so, what concepts of heaven or of afterlife have you previously held?

Watch Session 1
Intro Video Message

Who is God? That is a question we must be able to answer for ourselves. In order to pray in true, believing power, we must know the One whose touch we seek. To share our faith in Christ with others, we must be able to introduce them to our Father.

The one true God, the God Colton met in heaven, is the holy Trinity: God the Father, God the Son (Jesus), and God the Holy Spirit (Genesis 1:2–3; 2 Samuel 23:2–3; Job 33:4; Micah 5:2; John 1:1–3, 14; 8:58, 10:30; 15:26). He is real and personal and holy. So when we say, "God," we are not referring to a generic "higher power," or a god we've made up from our own wishes, but the holy God of heaven and earth, the Author of eternity.

It is a fact that God, in some form, however mistaken, is acknowledged by most; however, far too often, Jesus is invisible. The One who revealed to us the very character and nature of God (John 14:8–10), the One who died so that we could know the Father and live eternally with Him (John 17:3), is conspicuously absent from most aspects of society.

Group Discussion

✹ What thoughts do you have when you consider the nature of God as Father, Son, and Holy Spirit? Can you think of examples in God's Word, the Bible, that would enable you to better grasp this difficult concept?

✹ Have you noticed the absence of Jesus, even in places where God may be acknowledged? Does that trouble you? Why or why not?

✹ What are some examples of "gods" we try to create for ourselves? How do they stand up against the one true God we find in Scripture?

✹ Being totally honest, describe God's nature or value in your own experience.

✳ How important is it to be clear on God's identity?

Watch DVD Session 1

Just as it is important to know what we mean by "God," it's vital to know what we mean by "heaven." We are not talking about a hybrid destination that some religions call "nirvana," "becoming one with the universe," or "reincarnation" of some form or other. We are talking about the eternal home prepared by God for those who have believed in and followed Him, a home made available to us through the salvation provided by Jesus Christ, His Son. We're talking about everlasting closeness to God in the place where He has righted all wrongs and healed all wounds of this present world. Heaven is the fulfillment of God's kingdom and our life in Him.

Knowing the reality of this eternal home can be the life preserver that keeps our heads above water when life becomes overwhelming. Holding a biblically valid perspective can help us keep walking, even when the problems of the world challenge every step. We will spend eternity somewhere, so it is vital to think about, and know to our fullest ability, where that will be. In Colton's words, it is so important to know that "heaven is for real."

Scripture

- John 5:24–29:

"Most assuredly, I say to you, he who hears My word and believes in Him who sent Me has everlasting life, and shall not come into judgment, but has passed from death into life. Most assuredly, I say to you, the hour is coming, and now is, when the dead will hear the voice of the Son of God; and those who hear will live. For as the Father has life in Himself, so He has granted the Son to have life in Himself, and has given Him authority to execute judgment also, because He is the Son of Man. Do not marvel at this; for the hour is coming in which all who are in the graves will hear His voice and come forth—those who have done good, to the resurrection of life, and those who have done evil, to the resurrection of condemnation." (NKJV)

- Matthew 25:32–34, 41, 46:

  "All the nations will be gathered before Him, and He will
  separate them one from another, as a shepherd divides his
  sheep from the goats. And He will set the sheep on His right
  hand, but the goats on the left. Then the King will say to
  those on His right hand, 'Come, you blessed of My Father,
  inherit the kingdom prepared for you from the foundation
  of the world' . . . Then He will also say to those on the left
  hand, 'Depart from Me, you cursed, into the everlasting fire
  prepared for the devil and his angels' . . . And these will go
  away into everlasting punishment, but the righteous into
  eternal life." (NKJV)

- Romans 6:23:

  For the wages of sin is death, but the gift of God is eternal life
  in Christ Jesus our Lord. (NKJV)

Group Discussion

✹ Has what we've discussed in this session changed your view of heaven? If so, how so?

✹ How does your current view of heaven contrast with your prior concepts?

✹ What first intrigued you about Colton's story? What encouraging experiences have you already had or heard about, stemming from the sharing of his journey?

✽ How have you been strengthened to share your faith and your own stories?

✽ John 5:24–29 makes it very clear that we will all spend eternity somewhere—we will either live in eternal life or everlasting condemnation. How can knowing that eternal life, true life with God, is your ultimate future help you face the challenges you have on this earth? How does knowing the reality of unending condemnation for those who do not know Christ motivate you to share the truth of salvation and eternal security in Him?

✳ In Matthew 25, we see this truth shown even further. Heaven is the kingdom created for us "from the foundation of the world" (v. 34 NKJV). God prepared our eternal home before we even came into being. How does that fact affect the way you think about heaven?

✳ In light of John 5 and Matthew 25, why should we care about heaven?

Heaven Is for Real

✺ In the beginning of this session, we discussed how society
acknowledges God, yet tragically ignores Jesus. What does
Romans 6:23 tell us about the presence of God the Father
and Jesus when it comes to eternity? Who is the source of
our eternal life in heaven?

Prayer

Lord, we thank You for loving us enough to provide salvation
from our sins and to prepare an eternal home for us. We pray
that You will bless our study and allow Your Word to speak to
us, teach us, challenge us, encourage us, and renew us. We
thank You for the journey You've given to Colton and his family,
and for their faithfulness in sharing it. Please be with us as we
continue to encounter the reality of your kingdom.

Real Reflection

It is so difficult for us to even imagine the glorious world Colton visited. How can our limited human minds conceive of the eternal wonders of God?

Colton used the words he knew at the age of four to attempt to describe the incomparable beauty and indescribable majesty of our Father's kingdom. His experience is much like the apostle John's, recorded in the book of Revelation, as John attempted to convey sights and sounds that were beyond his understanding. The apostle knew that mere words could not fully communicate the awesome richness of heaven, so more than sixty times he described his experience using the comparative "like." (See, for example, Revelation 1:10, 13; 4:1, 6–7; 6:1; 8:8, 10.)

But through the eyes of a child, we have been given a glimpse of the sublime experience that awaits those who know the Son of God.

PERSONAL REFLECTION

Read Deuteronomy 4:29 and Matthew 7:7–8.

Seek Him and you will find Him! God is available and ready to meet you when you set your heart on seeking His face.

We may not be able to sit on Jesus' lap and know the feel of His tender touch. We may not be granted the joy of looking into the loving eyes of our Savior before the day He takes us home. It may be the other side of eternity that reveals to us the glory of God's throne. But Jesus tells us we can know Him now. Through prayer and studying His Word, we can have the unparalleled contentment of intimacy with the Lord. Our Savior promises that He will reveal Himself to those who seek Him. Spend time with the Lord. Learn the gentle timbre of His voice as He speaks to your soul. Begin to hear the very heartbeat of your Creator as you encounter the Author of life. Drink deep of the water of life that pours forth for all who come near to God's throne of grace. Experience the joy of looking deep into the eyes of the very Source of life and love—our eternal, triune God: Father, Son, and Holy Spirit.

POINTS TO PONDER

- What does it mean to discover intimacy with Jesus Christ as Lord?

- What steps can you take to make intimacy with Jesus a reality in your life?

- Are prayer and Bible study an important part of your life? How much time do you spend with the Lord each day? Does that amount of time accurately reflect His importance in your life?

- Write down the words that honestly describe your faith relationship with Christ.

  _____

  _____

  _____

- Write down the words that truthfully describe your relationship with His church.

  _____

  _____

  _____

- What is your reaction to the descriptors you've used in the previous two questions? If your relationships with the Lord and His church are not what you desire them to be, how can improve these relationships?

Journal

Bringing It Home

- Why should we care about heaven?

- Read Revelation 21:1–5, 23–27; 22:1–5. What do you learn from these passages?

- Describe how you see heaven.

- Who lives in heaven?

- What do you think it will be like to see Jesus for the first time?

- What do you think it will be like to see God for the first time?

- What are some things that happen to you that make you sad?

- What will it be like to be in a place where you are never sad?

- How do you get to heaven?

Family Prayer

Jesus, we thank You for our family. Thank You for creating a home for us today, and for creating a home for us in heaven that will last forever. Please bless our family, Jesus. Help us always remember how much You love us. Show us how best to love our family, even on days when it seems hard. Help us to know You better every day, and remind us of all the wonderful things You have done for us. Amen.

What Is Heaven Like?

We all have questions about what heaven is like; but trying to describe heaven is a lot like trying to describe New York City to someone from an ancient time. Heaven is beyond our world, outside our dimension. It is a spiritual realm, and we live in a physical one. We can only use our own limited words, knowledge, and experiences to communicate things that are beyond our physical world. Some things Colton saw during his visit to heaven have been the source of disagreement and much discussion. We understand that. All we can do is share what he saw in the best way we know. But there are certain truths about heaven that cannot be denied. In this session, we want to focus on those truths as Colton experienced them and, most important, as Scripture describes them.

Jesus said, "In My Father's house are many mansions; if it were not so, I would have told you. I go to prepare a place for you. And if I go and prepare a place for you, I will come again and receive you to Myself; that where I am, there you may be also" (John 14:2–3 NKJV). He also confirmed to us that His Father is our Father (Luke 11:2). What amazing truth: Jesus has prepared a place for us in our heavenly Father's house!

Colton's favorite place in God's house was His throne room. Colton sat there with God the Father, God the Son, and God the Holy Spirit. You may find yourself wishing you could experience that same presence of the one true God. You can! God's throne room is a place where all who believe on the name of Jesus are welcome. God has issued an open invitation to live forever with Him in His house; to accept, we must simply believe in Christ as our personal Savior. Jesus is the door to God's house, giving us entrance into our true home of pure joy, meaning, and purpose.

We can have discussions about particular details of heaven, such as the presence of animals or whether or not we will have wings, but the ultimate truth is that heaven is very real, and we can live there eternally with God.

Now let's go a little further in Colton's journey, exploring the Word of God as we find out even more about what heaven is like.

Group Discussion

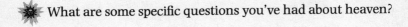 What are some specific questions you've had about heaven?

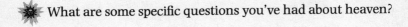 So far in our study, has the idea of heaven become more real to you? Why or why not? If it has become more real to you, in what way?

Watch Session 2
Intro Video Message

When considering what heaven is like, it is often tempting to be overwhelmed by complicated theories or details. Trying to describe an unknown place, much less a heavenly one, can be a massive challenge. We can get caught up in discussions about things such as streets of gold, or whether or not we'll see our pets there. And those aren't bad discussions. But perhaps the essence of what heaven is like doesn't have to be that complex. In the midst of all the details, what is it that truly defines heaven? Very simply, heaven is God's house. God's presence is there, and that is what makes heaven, heaven.

Genesis 1:27 tells us that we are created in God's image. But here on earth, it can be difficult to look in a mirror and see a reflection of the divine. It is easy to get caught up in our shortcomings, failures, and sometimes decidedly ungodly behavior. Yet, we are created in the image of God, and we are the very object of His affection (John 3:16). We were created by Him and for Him, so living eternally in His presence will be our ultimate fulfillment.

Heaven is meant to be our eternal home. As masters of our own homes, we do not grant entry to uninvited, unknown people; they cannot come in and do as they please. We welcome people into our homes who have requested entrance; we open our doors to those we know. We learn through God's Word that Jesus is the door to God's house and the only way into that perfect place (John 10:9). Heaven was prepared for us before the foundation of the world (Matthew 25:34), but entrance into that perfect place will be granted only to those who know heaven's Master, Jesus. None of us can follow our own road to heaven; neither can we map out our own strategies to gain entrance. There is no alternate door.

Jesus told us that He went to prepare a place for those who know Him, and that He will one day return to take them home with Him (John 14:2–3). No sin will be able to break in to God's house; it is not allowed through the door. But even though sin is a fact of all our lives (Romans 3:23), because of Jesus' love and sacrificial death on the cross, our sin is erased and heaven is available to all who will call upon the name of the Lord (Romans 10:13). To be assured of entrance into God's eternal kingdom, to know the perfect joy and peace of heaven, we need only to believe that Jesus is God's Son, that in dying for us He conquered sin, and that in rising from the grave, He conquered death. Through Jesus we can know eternal life in God's presence because Jesus said, "Where I am, there you may be also" (NKJV).

God's house is amazing—a home where no sin, shame, grief, or pain can follow us; an eternal dwelling into which we are all invited; a place where Love Himself rules. If sinful humanity can give and receive love, we can only imagine the love that pours forth from the One who is the very source of love. For you see, God *is* love (1 John 4:7–16), and all are invited to come to know Jesus and be granted entrance into God's timeless kingdom of love.

Group Discussion

☀ Have you previously thought of heaven as God's house? How can this image make heaven seem more personal to you?

☀ Why do you think Jesus chose to use the image of His Father's house to describe heaven?

✵ How does being reminded that you're made in the image of God affect the way you think of yourself? How does it influence the way you see God?

✵ Imagine what it will be like to live without sin and its effects. How will it feel to live without temptation? Without shame? Without the destructive consequences that sin always brings? In the place where Love Himself rules?

Watch DVD Session 2

Colton's experience of heaven was so tangible; it allows us a glimpse of heaven as a real place, and more important, as a real home. We will live there—really, truly *live*, not just exist as misty presences simply floating about in some otherworldly, vaporous place. Often, especially as children, we may imagine heaven to be a place where everyone sits on a cloud and plays a harp for eternity. But neither the Bible nor Colton's experience would have us believe anything of the sort. We will be happily busy in heaven. We will have purpose, meaning, and contentment. We will find ultimate fulfillment in the constant presence of our Father in His house, and experience total peace and joy in all we do . . . for eternity.

To our limited, human intellect, eternity is a nearly mind-boggling concept. God and His eternal kingdom exist outside of infinity, so heaven is a place without time. God is not constrained by the limitations of time and space, as we are. This helps us understand how Colton could have experienced so much in such a short time. On his journey, He visited a place beyond our finite time and space, so our hours, minutes, and seconds didn't apply. Just as the apostle Peter said, "With the Lord, one day is as a thousand years, and a thousand years as one day" (2 Peter 3:8 NKJV). Whether or not you apply that equation mathematically to the three minutes Colton spent on his journey, when you realize that heaven is in no way beholden to our clock, it is much easier to accept that so much happened in such a small segment of earthly time.

While describing details of heaven itself (such as colors, music, animals, or wings) is challenging, relating events outside of time is as well. Colton was able to see events from earthly past, present, and future. While it may be a bit disconcerting to hear your son tell you about a battle you're going to fight in your resurrected body, it is also inspiring to know that one day we will live in a place where time is no longer an enemy, or even an impartial participant, ticking off the moments of our lives.

Colton's visit to heaven has made Scripture become even more vivid and alive to our family; we hope it can do the same for you. We are reminded that we are not simply talking about concepts and stories in the Bible, but about real people and a real, personal God who has prepared a real, personal home for us. So when we see a rainbow, it's not just a beautiful reminder of a Sunday school story. Rather, it is an authentic reminder that we have a genuine God who keeps His promises. When we read in Psalms that we can trust in the shelter of His wings (61:4), we can be assured that we can trust Him completely. When the New Testament talks about having a peace that passes understanding (Philippians 4:7), we know that this is not just pretty language; it is a real peace from Jesus that can sustain us through the most trying of circumstances.

As we have discussed, heaven exists in an infinite realm outside of time and space. We cannot possibly know or comprehend everything about a place so far removed from our earthly experience. But the little we do know can help us realize that the mystery of heaven should excite and encourage us, not frighten or intimidate us. We don't have to look upon the mystery with fear, because we know that beyond it lies even more incredible, beautiful, and indescribable joy than we can imagine.

So let's go to Scripture and see what else we can learn about what heaven is like.

Scripture

● Matthew 13:44–46:

"Again, the kingdom of heaven is like treasure hidden in a field, which a man found and hid; and for joy over it he goes and sells all that he has and buys that field.

"Again, the kingdom of heaven is like a merchant seeking beautiful pearls, who, when he had found one pearl of great price, went and sold all that he had and bought it." (NKJV)

- Revelation 7:16–17:

  They shall neither hunger anymore nor thirst anymore; the sun shall not strike them, nor any heat; for the Lamb who is in the midst of the throne will shepherd them and lead them to living fountains of waters. And God will wipe away every tear from their eyes. (NKJV).

- Revelation 21:1–5:

  Now I saw a new heaven and a new earth, for the first heaven and the first earth had passed away. Also there was no more sea. Then I, John, saw the holy city, New Jerusalem, coming down out of heaven from God, prepared as a bride adorned for her husband. And I heard a loud voice from heaven saying, "Behold, the tabernacle of God is with men, and He will dwell with them, and they shall be His people. God Himself will be with them and be their God. And God will wipe away every tear from their eyes; there shall be no more death, nor sorrow, nor crying. There shall be no more pain, for the former things have passed away."

  Then He who sat on the throne said, "Behold, I make all things new." And He said to me, "Write, for these words are true and faithful." (NKJV)

- Revelation 21:10–11:

And he carried me away in the Spirit to a great and high mountain, and showed me the great city, the holy Jerusalem, descending out of heaven from God, having the glory of God. Her light was like a most precious stone, like a jasper stone, clear as crystal. (NKJV)

- Revelation 21:18–23:

The construction of its wall was of jasper; and the city was pure gold, like clear glass. The foundations of the wall of the city were adorned with all kinds of precious stones: the first foundation was jasper, the second sapphire, the third chalcedony, the fourth emerald, the fifth sardonyx, the sixth sardius, the seventh chrysolite, the eighth beryl, the ninth topaz, the tenth chrysoprase, the eleventh jacinth, and the twelfth amethyst. The twelve gates were twelve pearls: each individual gate was of one pearl. And the street of the city was pure gold, like transparent glass. But I saw no temple in it, for the Lord God Almighty and the Lamb are its temple. The city had no need of the sun or of the moon to shine in it, for the glory of God illuminated it. The Lamb is its light. (NKJV)

Group Discussion

Jesus often used parables (short, allegorical stories) to describe the kingdom of God. Heaven is the ultimate fulfillment of the kingdom of God, so the parables in Matthew 13 suggest that heaven is a treasure beyond comparing to anything we can have or know on this earth.

 What are some of your favorite things that Jesus tells us about heaven? Why are they important to you?

Romans 14:17 tells us that God's kingdom is a place of righteousness, peace, and joy. What experiences come to mind when you consider the word *joy*?

✸ Describe a time when you felt the most contented and
peaceful. What insight does that experience give you
into the "perfect peace" God gives (see Isaiah 26:3 NKJV)?
How does it encourage you to know that one day you can
experience that perfect peace eternally?

✸ Earlier, we discovered that what makes heaven, heaven
is God's presence. Colton's favorite place in heaven was
God's throne room. Revelation 21:3 makes it clear that we
may all one day experience His majestic, loving presence.
Describe a time when you felt especially close to God.
How does that experience help you imagine what an
unhindered, eternal experience of God's presence will be
like in heaven?

✹ Describe something you have seen in a state of destruction
or decay. What did you think or feel when you saw it?
Has there been a time in your life when you have felt the
crippling effects of devastation or despair? Revelation 21:5
tells us that God will make all things new. Heaven will be
a place of eternal newness, for our surroundings, and
also for us. How does this truth speak into the brokenness
you've encountered in your world or in your own life?

✹ Revelation 21 speaks of the light and city of heaven as
being as clear as crystal and glass (vv. 11, 18). What do you
think is the significance of such clarity and brightness?

✳ According to Revelation 21:23, what is the source of the light in heaven?

✳ What are some areas of your life now that need clarifying by the light of Jesus?

✳ If you had to answer the question, what is heaven like? in your own words, what would you say?

Prayer

Lord, we thank You for providing the way for us to experience Your presence now, and for eternity. Thank you for giving us purpose and peace, even on earth, but especially the perfect peace and everlasting fulfillment waiting for us in heaven. Thank You for the beautiful mystery of our eternal home. Please help us to appreciate all we can know now about Your house and to embrace through faith what we can't yet know. Help us to respond to your Word with the faith and trust that You have prepared incomparable treasures for us out of Your great love. Please continue to lead us in this study, as we seek to know more about You and Your house. Amen.

Real Reflection

When we think about and try to describe what heaven is like, we're often tempted to get bogged down in details or debates. While there's nothing wrong with details or healthy discussions, sometimes the more we complicate something, the more we miss the forest for the trees.

This may be one reason Colton's story has resonated so strongly with so many people. We get to live his journey through his preschool eyes and his pure, childlike faith. He saw what he saw, and because of that, he just wants to tell people that God really, really loves them.

In the video, Sonja mentioned a particular scripture becoming especially vivid to her through Colton's experience. Let's look a little more closely at this passage.

PERSONAL REFLECTION

Read Mark 10:13–16.

Childlike faith—it's not a difficult formula: believing, loving, and following God as His own child, trusting and worshipping as a little one without guile or self-consciousness. Reaching up to our Father and inviting His loving embrace, no matter what our age, is how we experience the kingdom of God today and eternally.

That's not to say that we should not devote ourselves to studying and meditating on Scripture to learn more about God and the ways of faith. We are called to love God with all our hearts, souls, minds, and strength (Mark 12:30). So there is a place for our minds in matters of faith. It is healthy to study and discuss the truths of God's kingdom. But we have limited minds, and hearts that can be deceived. At the end of the day, when it comes to faith, it is comforting to know that we can simply believe God's Word—rely completely on Him and what He's promised, and respond to His love with a childlike faith. When we see a rainbow, we can be reminded that God is the ultimate Promise Keeper. We can trust that heaven is real because our heavenly Father told us so. We can expect God to keep His promises because we can know His character through His revealed Word—the Bible. We can be confident that we can know Him now (Jeremiah 29:13), and that we will know Him even better in heaven (1 Corinthians 13:12). Jesus is with us today (Matthew 18:20), and we will know the ultimate joy of living in our Father's presence throughout eternity (Revelation 21:3).

POINTS TO PONDER

- Why do you think Jesus considered it so important that the children be allowed to come to Him?

- How would you define *childlike faith*?

- How can you balance earnest and serious Bible study with having faith like a child's?

- What is your biggest challenge when it comes to childlike faith? What is your biggest challenge with regard to balancing childlike faith and loving God with all of your mind?

- What steps can you take to begin to overcome those challenges?

- Before this study, did you ever stop and think about rainbows? What will you think of now every time you see a rainbow? What other signs of God's love and faithfulness do you see in the world around you?

- Jesus is God's Son. He came to die in your place and to free you from sin and death. Take time to read John 3:16 and Romans 10:9–13. If you do not know Jesus as your personal Savior, earnestly pray the prayer in the next section. Jesus died for everyone; more important, He died for you.

Journal

Bringing It Home

Read John 14:1–3.

- Jesus referred to heaven as His Father's house. Heaven will be a perfect place. What do you imagine God's house to be like? What will make it perfect?

- Jesus said He is preparing a place for us in His Father's house. Why do you think He's preparing it for us? What do you think Jesus might be doing to prepare for us?

Read Revelation 7:16–17.

- Can you imagine never feeling hungry or thirsty again? Why do you think we won't have those feelings in heaven?

- What things make you sad? How do you think it will feel to never be sad about anything?

- What do you think it means that God will wipe away all tears?

- What do you think "living fountains of water" might be?

- Is heaven a place you want to go when it's time? How do you think you get there?

Read John 3:16 and Romans 10:9–13.

● What do you think these verses mean?

If you want to know Jesus, you may pray the following prayer and be sure that He will hear you and answer. If you choose to pray and you really mean it, Jesus will become your own, personal Savior—He will help you live your life in ways that please God, and one day you can live with Him forever in God's wonderful house.

Prayer for Salvation

Father, I believe. I believe You sent Jesus to die for me and bring me life forever in Your kingdom. Please forgive me for doing wrong things. Help me live my life in ways that please you. I want to be Your child, and I want to live in Your kingdom today and be with You forever. Please accept me into your kingdom and give me new life in You. Jesus, please be Lord of my life and teach me how to be a faithful child of God. Amen.

Family Prayer

Jesus, thank You so much for preparing our home in heaven, Your Father's house. Thank You for loving us enough to return for us and take us to the home You are preparing for us. Until that time, please help us live our best for You here on earth. Help us to love You and to tell others about Your love. Lord, we pray that You will give us the right words to help others know You so that they, too, can live in Your Father's house. Amen.

When Does a Person Go to Heaven?

Heaven is the place you go when you die in the Lord, right? That's what I had always believed and accepted; but when Colton experienced heaven, he had not died. This fact confused me at first, until I remembered Paul's words about a "man in Christ" who was "caught up into Paradise" (2 Corinthians 12:2–4 NKJV).

In the time since Colton's return to us, I have often pondered his experience and marveled at the reality of heaven. To realize it exists *now*, in another realm, to recognize fully that it is a literal place, is the source of such hope and encouragement for our family, as well as those who have shared our experience through our book.

Colton makes no secret of his desire to return. But between now and the time he makes his repeat journey, there is a lot of life for him, and us, to live. Although we intend to live our lives for the Lord and do all He would ask of us here, we all feel a magnetic drawing toward our eternal home. It's hard to imagine anyone would not desire to live in the kingdom of God—to be in His presence and experience the joy only His kingdom can bring.

Though we desire heaven, the reality is that God's kingdom is available to us today. You see, His kingdom is a matter of "now" as well as "not yet." We will one day be transported to God's kingdom that is "not of this world" (John 18:36). But at the same time, we who know Jesus as Savior and Lord experience God's kingdom here on earth because Christ rules our lives, fills our hearts, and operates in power through us. Jesus said that the "kingdom of God is within you" (Luke 17:21). He did not mean that within ourselves we hold some divine quality, but Jesus Himself has taken up residence in the hearts of those who believe (John 17:23). The Spirit of God has been given to us (1 Corinthians 6:19), and we are called to live out the kingdom of God in this world. Romans 14:17 tells us that the "kingdom of God . . . is righteousness, peace and joy in the Holy Spirit."

Jesus taught us to pray, "Your kingdom come, your will be done on earth as it is in heaven" (Matthew 6:10). To enable us to live as children of the kingdom today, doing His will in the world, He sent the Holy Spirit. The Spirit brings: love, joy, peace, longsuffering, kindness, goodness, faithfulness, gentleness, and self-control (Galatians 5:22–23 NKJV). These are qualities of God's own nature at work in our lives. Through them, through us, God's kingdom is here and now. God will use us to point the way for others to know the reality of His eternal kingdom and to share the good news that heaven is for real.

Group Discussion

✹ In your understanding, what exactly is the kingdom of God?

✹ How do Jesus' words "the kingdom of God is within you" make you feel?

✺ Does the kingdom of God live through you? Why or why not?

✺ In your own words, explain the concept that the kingdom of God is both "now" and "not yet."

Watch Session 3
Intro Video Message

In a world that is more concerned with religion than with faith, we are often overtaken by the misconception that we must earn our right to enter heaven. What a dangerous and deeply flawed mind-set! In Psalm 14:2–3, David spoke clearly of our ability to be good enough to purchase our own entry into God's kingdom:

"The LORD looks down from heaven upon the children of men, to see if there are any who understand, who seek God. They have all turned aside, they have together become corrupt; there is none who does good, no, not one" (NKJV).

If we are honest with ourselves, we will own up to the fact that we are incapable of being truly "good." No one knows better than we ourselves just how sinful we can be in our thoughts and attitudes. But God has poured out mercy and grace through His Son. By His death, Jesus made a way for us to receive total forgiveness for sin so we could also obtain righteousness (right standing) in God's sight. Jesus has purchased our freedom with His blood, restored our relationship with our Father, and regained for us our eternal reward. We need only to repent, accept, and believe (Romans 3:21–26).

All of us, even those of us who have accepted Jesus as our Savior, struggle with sinful actions and attitudes (1 John 1:8–9). Just as I did when Colton's life was in danger, we can be overtaken by anger and fear; we may even lash out at God, showing Him disrespect and disdain. But God is not surprised by our actions or words; He is not impressed by our anger, and our fear does not cause Him dismay. God knows exactly what is in our hearts and minds even before we speak; He knows we are incapable of sinless lives (Romans 7:14–25). And God desires that we be honest and transparent before Him. Without honesty before God and willingness to confess our sin, we cannot receive His forgiveness. Without transparency and a readiness to admit our need, we will not receive the abundant life God longs to shower upon us.

Life can teach us to avoid truly disclosing our deepest selves. We fear rejection by others and therefore never allow them to see parts of us that may alienate us from them. But God sees us and knows our hearts before we give them voice, yet He loves us and forgives us in the midst of our ugly reality.

Group Discussion

✴ Has there been a time in your life when you had negative feelings toward God? Share your experience, if you are able.

✴ Read Psalm 139:23–24. What is your reaction? How does being transparent before God make you feel?

Are you confident that you will one day live in God's house—that heaven will be your eternal home? Why or why not?

If at this point you still lack confidence that you will one day live with God in heaven, here's what the Bible tells you to do to be sure: "If you confess with your mouth, 'Jesus is Lord,' and believe in your heart that God raised him from the dead, you will be saved. . . . 'Everyone who calls on the name of the Lord will be saved'" (Romans 10:9, 13).

Do you want to call on Him? If so, pray the prayer for salvation from Session 2.

Watch DVD Session 3

Jesus said, "In the world you will have tribulation; but be of good cheer, I have overcome the world" (John 16:33 NKJV). He did not say we *might* have trouble and sorrow; He said that hard times *will* come. That's because we live on a battleground—all around us a war is being fought between good and evil. We have an enemy who wants to destroy us only because God loves us (1 Peter 5:8). Satan will stop at nothing to try to defeat God's people or keep those who don't know God from finding His love and salvation.

When Colton's condition deteriorated, leaving him lifeless, exhausted, and filled with poison, I was desperate. I was angry at God; at the root of that anger was pure, cold, dreadful fear. I could not accept that my son was dying and I could do nothing to help him. So I called out to God in angry desperation. In utter fear, I raged at Him.

Jesus often told us we should not be afraid (Matthew 10:26, 28, 31; Luke 12:4, 32; Revelation 1:17). When fear overtakes us, it begins to rule our hearts and minds. We become obsessed with the negative "what-ifs" that tomorrow, or the next minute, may hold. Instead of trust, our hearts are filled with dread. Rather than hope, we become mired in hopelessness. When we allow fear to rule, we have ceased to operate in faith. Faith hopes; faith believes; faith trusts in God. Fear denies His love.

Even in my fearful rage, I realized my helplessness. Like the disciples, who, when asked by Jesus if they were going to leave him, answered, "Lord, to whom shall we go? You have the words of eternal life" (John 6:68), I knew that only the Lord could help my son and my family. Only He could restore life, bring comfort, and heal Colton. So I turned to Him in all my ugly humanity. And He heard my prayer!

Sometimes God answers prayers in the way we hope; sometimes He does not. We may not understand the reasons for God's actions or inaction, but we must "walk by faith" even when our lives seem to be falling apart (2 Corinthians 5:7–8 NKJV) and our hearts lay in shreds at our feet. We must come to the place where we can say along with Job, "Though He slay me, yet will I trust Him" (Job 13:15 NKJV).

When our world crumbles beneath us, we can only hold firmly to our Father's love and His promise of eternal life with Him. Though trials and sorrow may be inevitable in this world, we can know the powerful presence of God's kingdom within us today (John 16:33), and in the days to come, we will live with Him in a place where sin cannot enter and Love will always rule.

Scripture

- Isaiah 41:10:

  "Fear not, for I am with you; be not dismayed, for I am your God. I will strengthen you, yes, I will help you, I will uphold you with My righteous right hand." (NKJV)

- Isaiah 43:1–3:

  But now, thus says the LORD, who created you, O Jacob, and He who formed you, O Israel: "Fear not, for I have redeemed you; I have called you by your name; you are Mine. When you pass through the waters, I will be with you; and through the rivers, they shall not overflow you. When you walk through the fire, you shall not be burned, nor shall the flame scorch you. For I am the LORD your God, the Holy One of Israel, your Savior." (NKJV)

- John 16:33:

  "These things I have spoken to you, that in Me you may have peace. In the world you will have tribulation; but be of good cheer, I have overcome the world." (NKJV)

- 2 Timothy 1:7:

  For God has not given us a spirit of fear, but of power and of love and of a sound mind. (NKJV)

- Hebrews 11:1, 6:

  Now faith is the substance of things hoped for, the evidence of things not seen . . . Without faith it is impossible to please [God]. (NKJV)

Group Discussion

☀ Have you ever found yourself running from God during difficult times? If so, why, and what was the result?

☀ Isaiah 43 says, "*When* you pass through the waters . . ." and "*When* you walk through the fire . . ." It does not say "if." How do you feel knowing life will hold more trials for you?

☀ What steps do you believe you can take to face future trials with faith and not fear?

✴ What place do you believe humility holds in living a life of faith?

✴ Prayer is an act of faith and humility. What insights can you share about this statement?

✴ Do you find that you distance yourself from others in times of trial? Do you distance yourself from God? What is the result?

How can the body of Christ help during difficult times?

Do you have a story to tell that can encourage the faith of others? Can you share a bit of that now?

In what ways has this session changed the way you view the kingdom of God?

☀ What thoughts do you now have regarding the kingdom of God being both now and not yet?

☀ Are you assured that heaven will be your eternal home? Why or why not?

Prayer

Father, we praise You for Your limitless love. Thank You for sending Your Son to die for us so we can know life in Your kingdom today and the joy of Your presence for eternity.

Help us learn to live lives of faith and to trust in You even when life holds pain, illness, and loss. Use each of us, Lord, to encourage and strengthen others. Teach us how to live out Your kingdom on earth. Amen.

Real Reflection

It is important to realize that when we face trials, we are not alone. Jesus said, "I am with you always" (Matthew 28:20). And we have the promise of God: "I will never leave you nor forsake you" (Hebrews 13:5 NKJV).

PERSONAL REFLECTION

Read Proverbs 3:5; Psalm 4:4–5; 9:9–10; 18:30–31; 42:5; 62:5–8; 1 John 4:16; 1 Corinthians 2:9; Jeremiah 29:11–12.

My family walked through a year of one trial after another. We asked the same questions and expressed the same frustration that anyone would in those situations. We are not holier or any less human than anyone reading this book. The only foundation on which we could stand during those difficult days was Jesus and our strong belief in His limitless, constant love.

Before we can trust God through the trials that break our hearts and disrupt our lives, we must know that He loves us. Without that absolute knowledge, we cannot trust His plan for our lives when that plan takes us through pain and sorrow.

We are often asked why God chose to answer our prayers and spare Colton's life but has not responded in the same way to similar prayers for others. In answer, I can only say that God is always in control and we can trust Him to only act in ways that are best. God did not send Colton back to us because of any holiness or spiritual superiority on our part; God sent him back because of His love. What is so difficult to understand is that even if God *had* kept Colton in heaven, that, too, would have been an act of love. God cannot operate with any motivation except love because God *is* love. He doesn't *have* love or *give* love; love is the very substance of God's nature.

POINTS TO PONDER

- Do you firmly believe in God's love for you? How does that belief affect the way you face life's trials?

- According to Psalm 56:8, God is so deeply moved when His people suffer that He records their tears. He even saves them! What insight into God's nature does this picture portray?

- Jesus said, "He who has seen me has seen the Father" (John 14:9 NKJV). What attributes were apparent in Jesus when He walked the earth that can enable you to more realistically "see" God?

● Go to your favorite Bible and locate scriptures that give you insight into God's nature. Make a list of the attributes you find.

_____

_____

_____

_____

_____

_____

● In view of all the attributes you have discovered that describe God's nature, what reasons do you have for trusting Him even when life is painful and does not make sense?

Journal

Bringing It Home

- When does a person go to heaven?

- We can live our lives here on earth in ways that show others what heaven will be like. Name some things you can do that will help others understand how wonderful heaven will be.

- What do you think God is like?

- Why should we pray to God?

- Are you ever afraid? How can God help you through those times?

- In the Bible, Jesus said He came to show us what God is like. What are things about Jesus that help you understand God?

- Is it important to trust God even when difficult or sad things happen and you don't understand? Why do you think trusting God is important?

- The Bible says, "God is love" (1 John 4:16). What does that mean to you?

Family Prayer

Father God, we thank You for this time together to learn about You. Help our faith grow, and teach us to trust You at all times. We thank You for Jesus and for the love You have for us. Help us live our lives so others can see how much You love them. Give us the words and the opportunities to tell others about You and the wonderful kingdom of heaven where You live. We want to please You. Help us really understand what that means. Amen.

Where Is Heaven?

According to Scripture, Jesus "is seated at the right hand of the throne of the Majesty in the heavens" (Hebrews 8:1 NKJV). Jesus is right where Colton saw Him: in God's throne room, sitting at God's right side. But exactly where is that "throne of the Majesty"? Where is Jesus now, and how do we follow Him? By looking at the changes in Jesus after His resurrection, we may begin to see a picture of what we will experience when we leave the world behind and follow Jesus into our eternal home.

Let's take a look at what we know from God's Word.

After His resurrection, Jesus remained with His disciples for forty days (Acts 1:3). During that time, He appeared to many of His followers. He ate with them, talked with them, and continued to teach them about His Father's kingdom. He also possessed a body that looked much like everyone else's, except it was new; it was different. We know Jesus' appearance must have been a bit altered because Mary Magdalene recognized Him only after He spoke her name; and other followers spent hours with Him before they realized His identity. Apparently, He looked like Himself, yet different. We also know that He did some physically impossible things: He walked through walls (John 20:19, 26), appeared and disappeared at will (Luke 24:31), and defied gravity (Acts 1:9)!

On His last day with His disciples, He promised that He would always be with them and would provide power for them to live out their lives as His witnesses. Then He *rose*—He lifted up into the air and disappeared into the clouds! An angel spoke to His amazed disciples and promised that He would return in the same way (Acts 1:9–11).

So, Jesus rose into the air and was "taken up" into heaven—but exactly where did He go? Where is heaven?

When we consider the location of heaven, we immediately think in terms of direction—heaven is up. It is high above the earth, but exactly how high?

We have discussed the fact that God exists outside of space and time. In that state of being, location is not a relevant concept—it has to do with space. Rather, it may be more appropriate to think of heaven as a world beyond our own. A kingdom or dimension more real, more vibrant, more abundant, more fulfilling than our limited minds can grasp. A higher world, far above our current experience.

In Isaiah 66:1, God tells us, "Heaven is my throne, and the earth is my footstool." We are also told in 1 John 4:16 that "God is love." Love is enthroned in the kingdom of heaven. And that love is given freely to any who will receive. Regardless of heaven's exact location, God loves you and wants you to live there eternally.

Group Discussion

Why do you think Jesus was able to do things that are physically impossible for us?

Jesus rose into the air and disappeared into the clouds. What impact do you believe this may have had on those who witnessed it?

☀ What are the most difficult concepts for you to grasp when you consider the lack of space and time in heaven?

☀ God created heaven to be our eternal home; Jesus invited us to live there with Him forever. What feelings do these facts stir in your heart?

Watch Session 4 Intro Video Message

Monuments. memorials, statues—Washington, D.C., is filled with our country's best attempts to honor our nation's heroes and define our national identity. When we visit our homeland's seat of power, we are surrounded by reminders of the glory that is the United States. We are filled with gratitude, but humbled by the sacrifices given on our behalf. Our nation's capital is grand indeed; however, Washington's greatest efforts at grandeur and glory, while patriotically inspiring, still leave us as hollow as its marble halls. National patriotism gives us a way to live, but does not supply a reason.

Only in relationship with the Creator can we find reason and purpose. Only through the sacrifice of Jesus Christ can we discover the true freedom our hearts long to find.

And only in His presence can we realize our genuine identity, for "in him we live and move and have our being" (Acts 17:28). He is our homeland!

Heaven is the place Jesus prepared for us to celebrate life in Him forever. Monuments and marble halls cannot compare with streets of gold and the throne room of God. Nothing on this earth can compare to the eternal home Jesus has prepared for those who believe!

While we can easily find Washington, D.C., with a road map or a GPS, no GPS on this earth can give us the coordinates for heaven. But Jesus said that those who belong to Him already know the way. In fact, He went on to say, "I am the way" (John 14:4–6). Jesus came to lead us to our heavenly Father and to enable us to experience eternal life with Him in His kingdom.

But where is God's kingdom? Often in the Old Testament, especially in Psalms, we are told that God is our dwelling place

(Psalm 90:1; 91:9). Precisely where He is located or in what dimension, we cannot know. However, we know that we are "in Him," that we actually abide in Him, and that He is love (1 John 4:16). Whatever the exact locale of heaven, we know it exists in the center of God's love.

Group Discussion

☀ Have you ever visited a monument or memorial that impacted you? In what way?

☀ How did the actual experience measure up to your expectations?

✺ Do you ever experience anticipation of your eventual experience of heaven? How so?

✺ Heaven is more an experience than a place. Do you agree with that statement? What does that statement mean to you?

✺ What did Jesus mean when He said, "I am the way" (John 14:6)?

Watch DVD Session 4

Often in Scripture (NKJV), the things of God are referred to as being "above" (Colossians 3:1; Psalm 50:4, 144:7; Romans 10:6). Whether or not we are to understand "above" as an elevated, spatial location, we can only speculate. Not even Colton can say exactly where he was when he was in heaven. But he can tell you that an angel carried him up past the clouds.

So many aspects of Colton's journey make us ask along with Mary, "How can this be?" We can only echo Gabriel's response, "With God nothing [is] impossible" (Luke 1:34, 37 NKJV). So many details about eternity are unclear to us in this world. But one day, we will know even as we are known, and all our questions will be answered (1 Corinthians 13:12). For now, we can only glean the truth as it is presented to us in God's Word—the Bible.

For our family, Colton's experience created many questions. We turned to Scripture—our final authority—for answers and guidance. Following are some issues we encountered and the scriptural truths we discovered.

WINGS

There are many scriptural references to a variety of creatures in heaven, including people, that had *wings*. Here are some examples:

Then I looked up—and there before me were two women, with
the wind in their wings! They had wings like those of a stork.
(Zech. 5:9)

Hide me in the shadow of your wings. (Psalm 17:8)

How precious is Your lovingkindness, O God! Therefore the
children of men put their trust under the shadow of Your wings.
(Psalm 36:7 NKJV)

The four living creatures, each having six wings, were full of
eyes around and within. And they do not rest day or night,
saying: "Holy, holy, holy, Lord God Almighty, Who was and is and
is to come!" (Revelation 4:8 NKJV)

Colton says we will all be given wings in heaven. Even
though this seems like an incredible upgrade, the Bible doesn't
mention this as fact. But there is no scripture that clearly
objects either. The Bible is silent on this issue.

HEAVENLY BODIES

Colton saw only young people in heaven: his great-grandfather
(who died at age sixty-one, many years before Colton was
born) was a young man, without the glasses he wore on earth.
However, Colton's unborn, older sister seemed to be aging at
a normal "earthly" rate. Age is really a moot point in heaven
because heaven exists outside of space and time. Our heavenly
"age" will be the perfect one, as *all* things will be perfect in

heaven. According to Scripture, all earthly imperfections and infirmities will cease once we enter our eternal home.

> And I heard a loud voice from heaven saying, "Behold, the tabernacle of God is with men, and He will dwell with them, and they shall be His people. God Himself will be with them and be their God. And God will wipe away every tear from their eyes; there shall be no more death, nor sorrow, nor crying. There shall be no more pain, for the former things have passed away." Then He who sat on the throne said, "Behold, I make all things new." And He said to me, "Write, for these words are true and faithful." (Revelation 21:3–5 NKJV)

> So also is the resurrection of the dead. The body is sown in corruption, it is raised in incorruption. It is sown in dishonor, it is raised in glory. It is sown in weakness, it is raised in power. It is sown a natural body, it is raised a spiritual body. There is a natural body, and there is a spiritual body. . . . And the dead will be raised incorruptible, and we shall be changed. For this corruptible must put on incorruption, and this mortal must put on immortality. (1 Corinthians 15:42–44, 52–53 NKJV)

> Beloved, now we are children of God; and it has not yet been revealed what we shall be, but we know that when He is revealed, we shall be like Him, for we shall see Him as He is. (1 John 3:2 NKJV)

HEAVENLY "TIME"

We have discussed a bit about the absence of space and time in heaven. It's a concept so alien to our experience that it's hard to grasp, let alone communicate. Colton says he was in heaven for "three minutes," yet he experienced what could have taken weeks on earth. We also know that in heaven there is no sun or moon; God is the light there. There is nothing to mark time because time is not.

> But, beloved, do not forget this one thing, that with the Lord one day is as a thousand years, and a thousand years as one day. (2 Peter 3:8 NKJV)

> For a thousand years in Your sight are like yesterday when it is past. (Psalm 90:4 NKJV)

> The city had no need of the sun or of the moon to shine in it, for the glory of God illuminated it. The Lamb is its light. (Revelation 21:23 NKJV)

> There shall be no night there: They need no lamp nor light of the sun, for the Lord God gives them light. (Revelation 22:5 NKJV)

Read Genesis 1.

MARKERS

For our family, Colton's experience has raised many questions. One of these concerns is what Colton called "markers" in Jesus' hands and feet. Some historians claim it was the Roman practice in crucifixion to drive nails through the victims' wrists rather than the palms of the hands. The account in the gospel of John supports Colton's observation of pierced hands rather than pierced wrists.

> After he said this, he showed them his hands and side. The disciples were overjoyed when they saw the Lord. (John 20:20)

> Now Thomas (called Didymus), one of the Twelve, was not with the disciples when Jesus came. So the other disciples told him, "We have seen the Lord!"
> But he said to them, "Unless I see the nail marks in his hands and put my finger where the nails were, and put my hand into his side, I will not believe."
> A week later his disciples were in the house again, and Thomas was with them. Though the doors were locked, Jesus came and stood among them and said, "Peace be with you!" Then he said to Thomas, "Put your finger here; see my hands. Reach out your hand and put it into my side. Stop doubting and believe." (John 20:24–27)

Those who have studied death by crucifixion say one common cause of death was asphyxiation. The reason the Jewish leaders asked for Jesus' legs to be broken was to hasten death by making it impossible for him to support himself by pushing up with his feet for air. This would indicate that the majority of Jesus' body weight was supported by his feet, not by his hands. In this case, nails would not have torn through Jesus' hands.

Now it was the day of Preparation, and the next day was to be a special Sabbath. Because the Jewish leaders did not want the bodies left on the crosses during the Sabbath, they asked Pilate to have the legs broken and the bodies taken down. The soldiers therefore came and broke the legs of the first man who had been crucified with Jesus, and then those of the other. But when they came to Jesus and found that he was already dead, they did not break his legs. (John 19:31–32)

Group Discussion

✳ Why do you think God's kingdom (heaven) is beyond our total comprehension?

✳ According to 1 Corinthians 13:12, we now see as through a dim "mirror." What do you believe that means?

✸ How does it make you feel knowing that you will one day
know even as you are known by God? What do you think
that means?

✸ What do you think of having wings in heaven?

✸ How do you believe a spiritual body differs from a "natural"
or physical body?

❋ What do you think it means to "put on immortality" (1 Corinthians 15:53 NKJV)?

❋ How does the fact that God created the sun and moon give insight into time in God's kingdom?

❋ First John 1:5 says that "God is light." What are your thoughts on that?

✳ Second Peter 3:8 says, "With the Lord one day is as a thousand years, and a thousand years as one day" (NKJV). What do you believe that means?

Prayer

Father God, on this day, we cannot know You fully; but one day, we will. We know we cannot grasp the majesty and mystery of Your kingdom, but please reveal to us all we need to know for today. Thank You for making us Your children and for preparing a place for us to live with you forever. In Jesus' name we pray. Amen.

Real Reflection

We read in 1 Corinthians 13:12 that one day, in heaven, we will know as we are known. We will know because we will see. We will see God and His eternal kingdom. Colton saw these things and has encouraged us all with his experiences. He saw wings; he saw lights surrounding people; he saw vibrant people in their primes; he saw angels; he saw past, present, and future. But the thing that most impressed Colton was the overwhelming love of God. God's love is so big that it was a part of Colton's every experience in heaven. Colton was known and Colton knew—He knew God's love. Now He encourages everyone to know the overwhelming power of that love.

PERSONAL REFLECTION

Read Ephesians 3:17–19.

While we are living in the "now" of God's kingdom, our knowledge is limited. But though we are incomplete in our comprehension of the things of God, there are things we can know and experience. Heaven is the fulfillment of God's kingdom, but we do not have to wait for heaven to experience the power of God's love.

In Ephesians 3, Paul prays that his fellow followers of Jesus Christ will be able to comprehend the full measure of God's love.

He says that all followers of Christ (saints) can comprehend this love and that this understanding can actually go beyond mere knowledge. It is a matter of heart and spirit, not just of mind and intellect. We can know all about someone without ever having spent any time with that individual. We can know his or her name, background, and the things that person has done or said. But without a personal relationship, we really don't fully *know* that person. Comprehending the true width and length and depth and height of God's love is much the same way. Without experiencing a personal relationship with God, without engaging our hearts as well as our minds, we cannot truly know Him or fully know His love.

While the full experience of heaven will be far beyond anything we can imagine, we are not left to wait without any consolation. Instead, we can already begin to know God and to live in His kingdom. We can read His Word and spend time in prayer and conversation with Him. We can get to know Him personally; and through that, we can begin to comprehend His love on all the levels of understanding we possess. While we do see dimly now, we can still see. We can still experience God's love. As Paul told us in Ephesians, when Christ dwells in our hearts and we are rooted in love, we can begin to perceive how huge God's love is. We start to appreciate the profound truth in Colton's simple statement: "God loves us so much, so much."

POINTS TO PONDER

- Why do you think that, out of everything Colton experienced, he always comes back to talking about how much God loves us?

- We know that God's kingdom is both "now" and "not yet." How do 1 Corinthians 13:12 and Ephesians 3:17–19 help us understand this concept?

- Who is your favorite actor? Who is your best friend? What are the differences in your knowledge of these two people? With this in mind, what does it mean to know God?

- Why do you believe God chose to let us experience part of His kingdom here on earth while we await its total fulfillment in heaven?

- Have you experienced God's love personally? If not, what steps can you take to discover its reality for yourself?

Journal

Bringing It Home

- Where do *you* think heaven is?

- Jesus is sitting right beside God in heaven. What do you think He's doing there?

- Jesus died on the cross for you. That is a wonderful thing. But He also rose from the dead—He came back to life! When He did, He looked pretty much the same as before, but He could do marvelous, amazing things: walk through walls, disappear suddenly, and rise up into the air. Why do you think Jesus could do these things?

- We know heaven exists, but we can't see it until God allows us to. Colton went to heaven, but he didn't die. Why do you think God showed him heaven while he was still alive?

- Colton said that he could fly in heaven. Do you believe people in heaven can fly? If so, why do you think they do? What do you think that will be like for you?

- Colton wants to ask God why there are bugs on earth. What would you like to ask God?

- The Bible says, "God is light" (1 John 1:5). What do you think that means?

- "With God nothing [is] impossible" (Luke 1:37 NKJV). What kinds of things can God do?

- Do you know that God says we can actually know Him? He says all we have to do is really want to and ask Him and He will help us understand what He is like. What are some things you know about God now?

Family Prayer

Father, we thank You again for Your love and for creating heaven for us. It will be so wonderful when we live there with You. But until that day, please help us to live lives that are pleasing to You. Help us to love others and to help them see how amazing You are. Thank You for our family and for letting us all be part of Your family here on Earth and in heaven. We want to learn more about You every day. Thank You for teaching us about how big Your love is. Amen.

Who Goes to Heaven?

One evening, while Jesus walked the earth as a man, Nicodemus, a Pharisee, came to speak with Him. Nicodemus believed Jesus had come from God and recognized the power of God in His life. But what Jesus said to him was shocking: "Most assuredly, I say to you, unless one is born again, he cannot see the kingdom of God" (John 3:3 NKJV).

Nicodemus was confused. "How can a man be born when he is old?" he asked. "Can he enter a second time into his mother's womb and be born?" (v. 4 NKJV).

Nicodemus did not realize Jesus was speaking of a spiritual event, not a natural one.

Just as we are physically born into *this* world, we must be spiritually born into God's kingdom. By receiving this new spiritual life, we enter into a new realm; it is a new state of being in which we discover the "now" of God's kingdom and gain assurance of the "not yet." In the "now" we are saved from the penalty of sin and death by accepting Jesus' death on our behalf. And though it is "not yet," we are assured of eternal life in God's kingdom to come—heaven—where we will live in God's perfect presence through eternity.

But how does this new birth take place?

We learned earlier that Jesus said, "I am the way and the truth and the life" (John 14:6). Jesus is the way we find this new life—through Him we experience spiritual birth into the kingdom of God. In Romans 10:9, we learn that "if you confess with your mouth the Lord Jesus and believe in your heart that God has raised Him from the dead, you will be saved" (NKJV). Simply stated, if you believe that Jesus is the Son of God and that He died for your sins and rose again in victory over death, new life in Him is yours for the asking.

Who goes to heaven? Those who "confess" and "believe" in Jesus and the salvation available to all who will receive new life in Him.

You may ask about Colton's sister or other children who have not had opportunity to know and receive salvation through Jesus. How can they enter heaven? Salvation is needed only where sin exists. A child too young to know right from wrong cannot truly choose to sin. Jesus said, "Let the little children come to Me, and do not forbid them; for of such is the kingdom of God" (Luke 18:16). No doubt, that is why Colton said repeatedly, "Jesus really, really loves the children."

Group Discussion

✸ Can you relate to Nicodemus? In what way?

✸ Have you experienced the spiritual birth discussed in this session? If so, share a bit of your experience. If not, do you have any questions you would like answered?

✺ Have you ever confessed to others your personal relationship with Jesus? Was it difficult? Why or why not?

✺ Those who know Jesus as their Savior will one day live with Him and with God in heaven. Does this promise bring you comfort? In what way?

Watch Session 5
Intro Video Message

Many of us have experienced the loss of a loved one. We know the pain of separation and the sorrow of saying good-bye. Death can cause us fear and great heartache; it seems an irrevocable end. However, Colton's experience plays out in vivid reality the fact that for those who know Christ, death is not an end, but a beginning. Rather than seeking closure of lost relationships, we need to seek patience, for one day, we will be reunited with those we love in the kingdom of God.

Colton expresses his desire to return to heaven. His feelings must be much like Paul's. The apostle found it difficult to choose between life in Christ's service here and eternal life in heaven (Philippians 1:22–24). He said that to "live is Christ and to die is gain" (v. 21). Paul realized, as Colton does, that heaven is an amazing place of perfection, where we will be reunited with those who have gone before, but more important, we will be united with God.

First Thessalonians 4:13 says we do not grieve as those who have no hope, but rest in a certain hope of reunion—not only with God, but with those we love. Those who possess this hope have Christ's promise, "Peace I leave with you, My peace I give to you; not as the world gives do I give to you. Let not your heart be troubled, neither let it be afraid" (John 14:27 NKJV). Finding closure when we lose a loved one to physical death may bring a measure of peace, but that poor substitute cannot compare to the perfect peace that can be ours through faith in Jesus.

Group Discussion

☀ Have you ever experienced the seeming hopelessness of losing someone you love? What other feelings did you have?

☀ What got you through that time? Did you ever receive true peace? How?

What are your feelings about death?

 Do you truly see heaven as your home? If so, in what way? If not, why?

 In what ways can you relate to Paul's conflict—whether to remain here or go on to be with Jesus?

Watch DVD Session 5

By now, we hope you have come to understand that physical death is really a passage into life for those who know Jesus. We don't die and *leave* home; we pass from life to life and *go* home.

Here on earth, our temporary home, our lives become overtaken by cares. Our focus is often determined by each day's concerns and challenges. Even for those of us who know the salvation of Jesus, our focus can be divided and clouded by the distractions of life. We see "in a mirror, dimly" (1 Corinthians 13:12 NKJV). It can seem as though this world is the only true reality. But since Colton returned to us with his report of heaven, that spiritual kingdom is now the one that gains our concentration and defines true reality for our family.

Although we still get distracted by the circumstances of life, we now have a constant reminder that this world is only for a time. We need to keep our eyes focused on God's kingdom and cling to His promise rather than allow the cares of this life to weigh us down and defeat us. We now try to always keep those things of eternal significance before our eyes and alive in our hearts.

One of the most powerful things Colton has told us about heaven is that "the first person you will see is Jesus." Imagine! What is it like to look into the eyes that beheld creation before it was complete? What is it like to see the smile that can light a kingdom? To feel the embrace of the arms that stretched wide on the cross to save us? To feel the touch of the hands that were pierced? To hear the voice that echoes through eternity, "Come, you blessed of My Father, inherit the kingdom prepared for you from the foundation of the world" (Matthew 25:34 NKJV)?

What a glorious way to step into eternity!

Scripture

- Philippians 3:12–14:

  Not that I have already attained, or am already perfected; but I press on, that I may lay hold of that for which Christ Jesus has also laid hold of me. Brethren, I do not count myself to have apprehended; but one thing I do, forgetting those things which are behind and reaching forward to those things which are ahead, I press toward the goal for the prize of the upward call of God in Christ Jesus. (NKJV)

- Hebrews 12:1–2:

  Therefore we also, since we are surrounded by so great a cloud of witnesses, let us lay aside every weight, and the sin which so easily ensnares us, and let us run with endurance the race that is set before us, looking unto Jesus, the author and finisher of our faith, who for the joy that was set before

Him endured the cross, despising the shame, and has sat down at the right hand of the throne of God. (NKJV)

- Matthew 6:25–34:

"Therefore I say to you, do not worry about your life, what you will eat or what you will drink; nor about your body, what you will put on. Is not life more than food and the body more than clothing? Look at the birds of the air, for they neither sow nor reap nor gather into barns; yet your heavenly Father feeds them. Are you not of more value than they? Which of you by worrying can add one cubit to his stature? So why do you worry about clothing? Consider the lilies of the field, how they grow: they neither toil nor spin; and yet I say to you that even Solomon in all his glory was not arrayed like one of these. Now if God so clothes the grass of the field, which today is, and tomorrow is thrown into the oven, will He not much more clothe you, O you of little faith? Therefore do not worry, saying, 'What shall we eat?' or 'What shall we drink?' or 'What shall we wear?' For after all these things the Gentiles seek. For your heavenly Father knows that you need all these things. But seek first the kingdom of God and His righteousness, and all these things shall be added to you. Therefore do not worry about tomorrow, for tomorrow will worry about its own things. Sufficient for the day is its own trouble." (NKJV)

Group Discussion

※ What are your thoughts regarding the fact that we don't *leave* home when we die in the Lord, but we *go* home?

※ What are some distractions in your life that cause you to lose focus on the fact that heaven is the true reality?

✹ What steps can you take in your own life to guard against being distracted by the cares of this world?

✹ What do you think your feelings will be when you first see Jesus with your own eyes?

✹ What do you think His first words to you will be?

✻ What do you see when you look at the drawing of Jesus in the book?

✻ Has this study caused you to feel more compelled to share your faith with others? In what way?

✻ Colton was able to see the past, the present, and the future from heaven. With this in mind, what do you believe the writer of Hebrews meant by the statement "We are surrounded by so great a cloud of witnesses" (12:1 NKJV)?

✳ What do you think "Seek first the kingdom of God" means? (See Matthew 6:33 NKJV.) How can you practice that in your own life?

Prayer

Father, You are so worthy of all our praise. Nothing we have to give can express our gratitude. You created us; You loved us in spite of our sinful selves; You saved us; You prepared an eternal paradise for us—You desire to have us with you for eternity! You are the Creator of the universe; nothing exists without You, yet You love sinful humanity with an intensity we cannot comprehend. Thank You for making the way for us to have a relationship with You. Amen.

Real Reflection

Jesus wanted us to understand God's kingdom. However, the things of God are so far beyond our world that it can be difficult to grasp them. That's why Jesus taught in parables (stories about common things that explain or define the uncommon)— to help us understand things about God and His kingdom.

Jesus spoke often about heaven. He wanted to remind us that this world is not our home. He wanted us to look beyond the trials and pain we might find in this world and keep our eyes on the things that have eternal significance. Not that Jesus does not understand the pain we experience in this world; as a matter of fact, in Psalm 56:8, we read that God actually records our pain and cherishes our tears. He cries them with us.

PERSONAL REFLECTION

Read Matthew 13:1–9, 18–23, 44–46.

POINTS TO PONDER

- What painful life experiences have come to mind during this last session? What were your feelings toward God during those sorrowful times? What are your feelings now?

- As you read Matthew 13:1–9, which type of soil best describes you? Why?

- What is the hidden treasure spoken of in Matthew 13:44? Do you own this treasure? Explain.

- In what way is heaven like a "pearl of great price" (v. 46 NKJV)?

- What have you learned in this study that has been life changing? How do you now view heaven?

- What aspects of heaven, as Colton experienced it and as Scripture has presented it, have most captivated you? Why?

Journal

Bringing It Home

- Who goes to heaven? Why do you think this is true?

- Now that we've reached the end of our study, do you know how you can be sure that you will live with Jesus in God's house (heaven)?

- Jesus said, "Let the little children come to Me, and do not forbid them; for of such is the kingdom of God" (Luke 18:16 NKJV). When Colton came back from heaven, he kept telling everyone, "Jesus really, really loves the children." Why do you think Jesus loves kids so much?

- What do you think "peace" means?

- The Bible tells us that Jesus will give us peace that is deeper than we can ever understand, even when we lose something or someone we love. What do you think that kind of peace feels like?

- Heaven is "perfect." Having completed this study, do you understand what that statement really means?

- What does the word *death* mean to you? Does that frighten you? (Parents, if your children are also participating in this study, please consider each child's maturity level before allowing him or her to watch this session's DVD with you.)

- Why should Colton's time in heaven help us not be afraid of death?

- What about heaven are you most looking forward to?

- What do you think it will be like to see Jesus?

- Do you think He will know you? Will you know Him?

Family Prayer

Father God, life can be so wonderful, but sometimes it's really hard. We thank You for the good times and ask You to help us with the hard ones. Help us always remember that You created a place for us to live with You where there will be no more hard times. We want to help others know all about You and what it's like in heaven. Please give us the courage to tell others about You and Your amazing love. Amen.

Conclusion

Taken from Revelation 22 (NKJV)

And he showed me a pure river of water of life, clear as crystal, proceeding from the throne of God and of the Lamb. In the middle of its street, and on either side of the river, was the tree of life, which bore twelve fruits, each tree yielding its fruit every month. The leaves of the tree were for the healing of the nations. And there shall be no more curse, but the throne of God and of the Lamb shall be in it, and His servants shall serve Him. They shall see His face, and His name shall be on their foreheads. There shall be no night there: They need no lamp nor light of the sun, for the Lord God gives them light. And they shall reign forever and ever.

Then he said to me . . . "Behold, I am coming quickly, and My reward is with Me, to give to every one according to his work. I am the Alpha and the Omega, the Beginning and the End, the First and the Last." . . . And the Spirit and the bride say, "Come!" And let him who hears say, "Come!" And let him who thirsts come. Whoever desires, let him take the water of life freely . . . He who testifies to these things says, "Surely I am coming quickly." Amen. Even so, come, Lord Jesus! The grace of our Lord Jesus Christ be with you all. Amen.

ABOUT THE BURPOS

TODD BURPO is the pastor of Crossroads Wesleyan Church in Imperial, Nebraska (Population: 1,762 in 2008), where his sermons are broadcast locally every Sunday via the local radio station. He also works at Chase County Public Schools as a wrestling coach for junior and high school students, as well as serving as a member of the school board. In emergencies Todd can be found working shoulder-to-shoulder with the Imperial Volunteer Fire Department as a fire fighter. He is also the chaplain for the Nebraska State Volunteer Firefighter's Association. To support his family, Todd also operates a company called Overhead Door Specialists. Todd graduated from Oklahoma Wesleyan University in 1991 *summa cum laude* with a BA in Theology. He was ordained in 1994.

SONJA BURPO is a busy mom to Cassie, Colton, and Colby and works at Moreland Realty as Office Manager. With a BS in Elementary Education from Oklahoma Wesleyan University and a Masters in Library and Information Science, Sonja is a certified teacher in the state of Nebraska. She has taught in the public school system both in Oklahoma as well as in Imperial. Sonja is passionate about children's ministry and also works side by side with Todd as administrator for his garage door company.

More information at
www.heavenisforreal.net
and
www.hifrministries.org

ABOUT LYNN VINCENT

LYNN VINCENT is the *New York Times* best-selling writer of *Same Kind of Different as Me*, the story of the unlikely friendship between a wealthy white art dealer and a homeless African-American man; and *Going Rogue: An American Life*, the memoir of former Alaska governor and vice presidential candidate Sarah Palin.

The author or coauthor of nine books, Vincent worked for eleven years as senior writer, then features editor, at the national news biweekly WORLD Magazine where she covered politics, culture, and current events. A U. S. Navy veteran, Lynn is also a lecturer in writing at the World Journalism Institute and at The King's College in New York City. She lives in San Diego, California.

For more information, visit *www.LynnVincent.com* or *www.Facebook.com/LynnVincentonFB*.

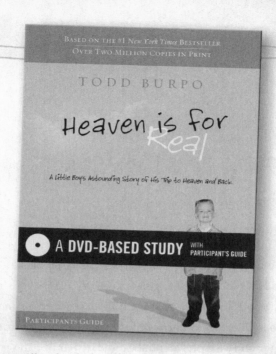

The best-selling book about heaven that has changed the world is now a DVD-based curriculum for churches and small groups. In addition to learning more about what the Bible teaches about heaven, groups will hear first-hand from the Burpo family about Colton's experience in heaven and the way it has changed their lives. Each video session features Todd, Sonja, and Colton, and is filmed interview-style with Natalie Tysdal, the Denver FOX/CW News reporter whose initial interview with the family has gone viral on the internet.

The Participant's Guide (ISBN 978-1-4185-5068-4) will take group members through key Bible passages about heaven, helping them understand more about who goes to heaven, when they go there, and what heaven is like.

More Information at *www.heavenisforreal.net*

Share the same comfort and assurance you received from *Heaven is for Real* with your children!

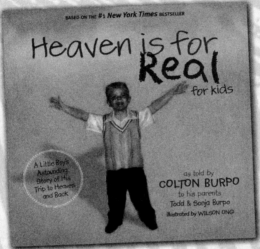

Uniquely written from a child for a child, *Heaven is for Real for Kids* is Colton Burpo's telling of his trip to Heaven. Colton shares a very important message that will speak to every child's heart... **"Jesus really, really loves the children!"**

Beautifully illustrated, the book also includes a Question and Answer section helping kids understand what the Bible says about heaven.

More information at www.heavenisforreal.net